my 3 angels

RODNEY TIMMS

TATE PUBLISHING
AND ENTERPRISES, LLC

Published by Tate Publishing & Enterprises, LLC
127 E. Trade Center Terrace | Mustang, Oklahoma 73064 USA
1.888.361.9473 | www.tatepublishing.com

Tate Publishing is committed to excellence in the publishing industry. The company reflects the philosophy established by the founders, based on Psalm 68:11,
"The Lord gave the word and great was the company of those who published it."

Book design copyright © 2013 by Tate Publishing, LLC. All rights reserved.
Cover design by Joel Uber
Interior design by Joana Quilantang

Published in the United States of America

ISBN: 978-1-62510-977-4
Biography & Autobiography / General
13.07.25

Dedication

I dedicate this book to my wife's parents. When we were talking about getting married, they could have run me off. They chose to do the right thing. They loved us.

They are the two most perfect people in this world. They don't tell you how to live; they *show* you.

I also dedicate this book to my first grandchild, Shelby Nicole Timms. I tell everyone, "As bad as my life was, as of November 3, 1998, I would not go back and change anything if it would have caused me to miss this precious child." I love all my grandchildren very much.

Also, I dedicate this to my wife and kids who unknowingly were my inspiration to try my best to do the right things in life. They will never know my personal struggles but have loved me for what I am today. Thank you very much!

1-800-4-A-CHILD
www.callingallhearts.com

Dedicated to my grandchildren

Shelby Timms
Ryan Timms
Ryder Southard
Cody Wilson
Hannah Spurgeon
Hattie Spurgeon
Hailey Spurgeon

We all love God and know we have
a purpose to help people!

In Jesus's name,
Amen

Acknowledgments

I'd like to thank my Creative Project Director, Jessica Huffman, for all the help on this project. She is an angel. This book would have never been written if it weren't for her. I thank God for her. I have been trying to write this book for the last fifteen years. Thank you, from the bottom of my heart.

I'd also like to thank my three angels. Without all of you, I would not be here today.

1-800-4-A-CHILD
www.callingallhearts.com

See that you do not look down on one of these little ones. For I tell you that their angels in heaven always see the face of my Father in heaven.

Matthew 18:10

For he will command his angels concerning you to guard you in all your ways.

Psalm 91:11

1-800-4-A-CHILD
www.callingallhearts.com

Foreword

When a child has been abused or neglected, the world can feel cold, empty, and alone. Time and time again when we speak with little survivors, we encounter children who have been blessed with angels in their lives that shepherd them through the darkest days. Childhelp champion Rodney Timms has been a guardian angel for the recovering children in our care, and it is fitting that he found his wings through being sheltered by angels of his own.

This stirring biography, *My Three Angels*, tells the story of a man who has seen some of the worst abuse imaginable but who transformed his broken spirit into a beacon of hope for others. The beatings began when he was just a baby, and he grew to watch his siblings experience equal cruelties. His mother tried to hide the bruises and battery, but she could not erase the damage of self-esteem and the brutal injuries to a young man's heart.

Timms writes, "The pain was absolutely unbearable. I honestly believed I was going crazy. Every night I begged God to help me."

As Rodney grew up, he lashed out the only way he was taught: in anger and violence. As we have discovered through a lifetime of advocating for abused children, hatred can be unlearned if a spirit is nurtured with love. Discover how three remarkable angels changed Rodney Timms's life and helped

1-800-4-A-CHILD

www.callingallhearts.com

him find his voice through poetry, prose, and public service. This is not the tale of a boy broken by abuse; it is the story of a man made whole through the grace of God—and a few earthly angels along the way!

Sara O'Meara
Childhelp Chairman & CEO

Yvonne Fedderson
Childhelp President

About Childhelp

CEO and Co-Founder Sara O'Meara and President and Co-Founder Yvonne Fedderson started Childhelp in 1959, establishing it as a leading national nonprofit organization dedicated to helping victims of child abuse and neglect and at-risk children. Childhelp's approach focuses on advocacy, prevention, treatment, and community outreach.

The Childhelp National Child Abuse Hotline, 1-800-4-A-CHILD, operates twenty-four hours a day, seven days a week, and receives calls from throughout the United States, Canada, the U.S. Virgin Islands, Puerto Rico, and Guam. Childhelp's programs and services also include residential treatment services; children's advocacy centers; therapeutic foster care; group homes and child abuse prevention, education, and training. Childhelp also created the National Day of Hope, held each April during National Child Abuse Prevention Month, that mobilizes people across America to join the fight against child abuse.

For more information about Childhelp, please call 480-922-8212 or visit www.childhelp.org.

1-800-4-A-CHILD
www.callingallhearts.com

Preface

Did you know…

- 90% of all prison inmates were abused in some form or fashion.
- 95% of all mental health problems are caused by abuse.
- In 2011, Oklahoma ranked third in the nation, behind New York and Mississippi, for child abuse and neglect deaths.
- 2 out of every ten girls are sexually abused by the age of 13.
- 1 out of every ten boys is sexually abused by the age of 13.
- 1 out of every five boys is sexually abused by the age of 18.
- 48% of abused children are boys.
- 52% of abused children are girls.
- 45% of abused children are white.
- 22% of abused children are African American.
- 22% of abused children are Hispanic.
- Abuse and neglect of American children have increased 134% since 1980.
- Physical abuse has increased 84% since 1980.
- Sexual abuse has increased 350% since 1980.
- Emotional abuse has increased 33% since 1980.

1-800-4-A-CHILD
www.callingallhearts.com

- Child neglect abuse has increased 320% since 1980.
- Every thirteen seconds a child is abused.

If these statistics do not move you, maybe this story will.

Five-year-old Shana's father taped her eyes shut during drinking bouts and gave her to his buddies to use as a sex toy. Suffering from trauma and reattachment disorder when rescued by the Oklahoma Department of Human Services (DHS), Shana soon found a stable home when foster parents Robert and Katherine B. adopted her.

At eight years old, she came across a handgun locked in a pickup truck and shot Robert through the hand while he was napping to, as she impishly put it, "see what it felt like." She stabbed cats with butcher knives and lured a two-year-old child away from her home with the intent to murder her. Robert and Katherine locked their bedroom door at night for fear the damaged little girl would kill them in their sleep. Finally returned to DHS for psychiatric treatment, Shana attempted to poison staff workers by pouring Drano into their tea. She is now in the custody of juvenile authorities until she turns eighteen.

In June 2011, five-year-old Serenity Deal died of a savage beating after DHS removed her from the custody of her mother and placed her with her father. The father, Sean Devon Brooks, has been charged with first-degree murder. Four long-time DHS workers were fired or suspended over having vouched before a judge that Brooks's home was a safe environment.

1-800-4-A-CHILD
www.callingallhearts.com

The mother of seventeen-month-old Ahonesty Hicks admitted smoking cigarettes laced with PCP when her boyfriend killed the little girl in May 2011.

Lyndsey Dawn Fiddler confessed to using morphine and meth when she drowned her ten-day-old daughter Maggie May in November 2010 by tossing her into the spin cycle of her washing machine.

Tulsa Oklahoma County Sheriff Stanley Glanz has stated, "The 'family' is disintegrating. The church community isn't as large as it once was. What we have is an increase in parents who simply don't care, and much of that is due to drugs, especially amphetamines."

There are an estimated twelve million cases of child abuse each year. Only a third of those ever get reported. We lose five children per day that are killed as a result of child abuse. Eighty percent of those are under four years of age.

Of the four million cases of reported child abuse, less than 1 percent ever makes it to court.

Don't you think it's time these laws were changed? They need to be changed by not giving people the ability to walk away from child abuse with a slap on the hand.

Remember, every thirteen seconds a child is abused.

My pleading to the world would be to please open your eyes to child abuse whether it is mental, physical, or sexual! It is making monsters out of our children! It's destroying lives right in front of our eyes.

My biggest problem while growing up was the fact that my dad was so violent toward me, my sisters, and my mother while fooling everyone else. We were threatened with our lives if we said anything to anyone about what a monster he really was. When my dad was around other people, he was a "good old boy." Everybody thought he was a great guy, when on his own turf he was a monster ready to kill. Most people never saw that side of him. I have friends and family that to this day don't believe he was that way. It would have scared them to death if they had seen the real him!

Worse than that was that our mother, time after time, had the opportunity to get us out of there. Because of pride, she would not do it. She did not want her family to know anything about it. I guess some didn't and still doesn't believe it.

My first chance at helping abused children was being a board member for the CARE Center in Oklahoma County. I was asked by the director to tell my story in a studio so it could be taped along with three women's stories. So I did just that. At the end of the tape, we had my three-year-old granddaughter come to me and get into my lap. I said, "Can you imagine abusing a child this precious, but it goes on every day. We need your help to stop child abuse." Once it was produced, I got copies of the tape and sent them to every relative and friend I had, asking them to help raise money for child abuse prevention.

After I sent them out, my mother called me one evening and asked, "What do you think you're doing?"

I replied, "What do you mean?"

She said, "You know what I mean! You sent that tape to Helen!" (Helen is her half-sister.)

1-800-4-A-CHILD
www.callingallhearts.com

I then stated, "I sent that tape to everybody for the purpose of raising money."

She then told me, "You are a no good son of a bitch because you can't forget!"

I replied, "Mother, I'm not ever going to forget that, and I'm damn sure not ever going to forget you *never* did anything to try to stop it!"

She yelled back, "Well, that doesn't matter!"

I heatedly replied, "The hell it doesn't!"

So she proceeded to tell me, "You can just go to hell and stay there!"

I then stated, "Mother, I'm not the one who's going to hell!" She hung up on me and hasn't spoken to me in the last ten years. I pray for my mother daily.

The other point I want to make is it is time for our churches to quit resting on their laurels! They have the key to stop this. Everybody keeps saying if God wants it fixed He will fix it. I have bad news folks: God has done all He's going to do. He is waiting on us to unite and stop it, as well as heal the sick. We have to stop just sitting in church. It's time to get up and do something. That also includes me! I'm just as guilty as the next person for sitting on my hands.

People, please unite, and let's stop making monsters, murderers, and mentally challenged people. We are letting people steal their lives. I need your help. I'm tired of turning on the TV every night to see another child abused or killed because of it! I am running out of tears. It breaks my heart!

1-800-4-A-CHILD
www.callingallhearts.com

Staggering to me is the fact that in 2011 Oklahoma was third in the nation in child abuse deaths! This is unacceptable! (We trailed only New York and Mississippi.)

For the most part, I made it! I am a survivor! It's a fact that only about 10 percent ever survive child abuse. Even the ones who do survive have "scars" that sometimes make it difficult for us to function. I am acquainted with a lady who is an extremely successful National Sales Rep for one of the large auto parts manufacturers that is a survivor. She says there are still times when she cannot get out of bed for days at a time due to her "scars."

If you or anyone you know has abuse trouble, please call 1-800-4ACHILD. Any type of child abuse can be reported to this number.

Make no mistake, God loves you, and He always will! Make a move toward Him. He's waiting on you! In Jesus's name, amen.

Wake Up and Look Around It Is Time to Stop Child Abuse

Introduction

I was born in 1953 in the tiny town of Frederick, Oklahoma. Frederick is the County Seat of Tillman County, located in the southwestern part of the state, about fifteen miles north of the Red River. Frederick has always been an agricultural town, not holding more than about five thousand people at any given time.

From an outsider, the town is idyllic. Frederick is very beautiful, full of small-town charm. In the middle of the town, there are rows and rows of Bradford pear trees, encircling the stately old courthouse and square.

I grew up on the southeast side of the town in a little frame house, not more than eight hundred square feet. The house was gray and was trimmed in white. A two-rail white fence encompassed it. At three years old, it wasn't much higher than me. The yard was small and was directly in front of a vacant lot that was always overrun with tall weeds.

To the west side of the house, there was a little one-car garage that stood at the south end of the driveway. I remember it always being full of *stuff*. There was a workbench hidden somewhere in the back, with a small path carved in all the junk straight to it.

I remember my dad making a spider out of copper wire and running a wire from the workbench to the door up through the ceiling so he could let the spider down in front of your face when you walked in the door. He seemed to really enjoy scaring people. Behind the garage was a chicken pen that we kept a few chickens in for our own consumption.

Our neighbors to the west were the Jeffcoats. They had two boys whom I played with at times. Their dad was a Holiness preacher, so my mom and dad wouldn't have much to do with them. Our neighbors to the east had a huge house and an even bigger yard. An elderly couple, the Johnsons, lived there. They were very kind to me, always making me peanut butter and jelly sandwiches and taking time to visit with me. They had a grandson my age, and when he would visit, we'd play Cowboys and Indians.

Across the road was the Kimbell family. Their two boys, Ronnie and Jerry, were my friends. Jerry was my age and therefore my best buddy. Ronnie was about three years older than Jerry and I, and he looked out for us. Their dad, Eugene, like my dad, drove a truck back then. Sadly, Ronnie and Jerry would die tragically in their later years in horrific truck accidents.

Across the street east of the Kimbell family lived the Hendricks family. They had two boys named Jimmy and Jerry. Jerry was also my age, and Jimmy was two years older. I remember Jimmy having a big bicycle, and it didn't have a chain protector on it, and he was always getting his pant leg caught in the chain. He was always riding really fast, and when his pants got caught in the chain, there would be a big crash.

1-800-4-A-CHILD
www.callingallhearts.com

People from the neighborhood would always gather around him to watch him try to get his pant leg out of the chain. It was a sight to see all the people completely surround him and watch him. No one ever offered to help him. Farther on down the street lived the Bobo family. Steve and Mark Bobo were about my age, and it seemed like such a long way to their house for a three-year-old.

Yes, the little town of Frederick and my neighborhood seemed like the quintessential small town. For me, however, it was something much darker.

Rodney

My name is Rodney, and this is my story,
And some of you may choose to ignore it.
I'm hiding under the bed,
Hoping he doesn't hit me in the head
Because last night when he did, I bled.

Do you think he will stop someday,
Or will I always be in the way?
When asked about all the bruises,
I no longer know what to say.

1-800-4-A-CHILD
www.callingallhearts.com

I've never felt pain like this,
Ever in my whole life.
What must I have done
To cause all this strife?

What in the world did I do
To make him so terribly mad?
My God, I'm only three;
What could I have done so bad?

Oh please, where are the people
To protect me from him?
Oh no, they are turning their backs!
Oh, I see, it's not hurting them.

1-800-4-A-CHILD
www.callingallhearts.com

Chapter One

I was up before the rooster crowed. It was Saturday; I only knew that because Shirley was still in bed and not getting ready for school. I decided to be bold and sneak downstairs to watch cartoons.

Me and my sisters' bedroom was right next to my parents' room, so I knew I'd have to be as stealthy as possible. I tiptoed as lightly as a kid can and finally made it to the living room.

I clicked on the old black-and-white television set and sat down, feeling a sort of victory that I had made it downstairs, undetected. Suddenly, I heard the front door swing open and slam. I jumped, clicked the television off, and tried to run up the stairs. I knew who was about to come in.

"Boy!" my father called behind me as I reached the bottom step. I stopped in my tracks. "Go wake your sisters and tell them to get down here, *now!*"

I didn't wait for any more instruction. I raced up the stairs and shoved the bedroom door open.

"Shirley! Carolyn!" I called, shaking my sisters. "Get up!"

"Go away, Rodney." Shirley moaned, shoving me away. "It's Saturday."

"But Shirley, Daddy wants us downstairs," I said hurriedly.

Shirley sat up straight, and Carolyn rolled off the bed. As quickly as we all could, we threw on the nearest pair of jeans and shirts we could find and raced down the stairs. I was

1-800-4-A-CHILD
www.callingallhearts.com

going so fast, I fell down the last two steps, but I hurried next to my sisters.

We stood there, like soldiers at attention, waiting for orders from our general. "I want this house cleaned up, and I want it done *now!*" He growled.

"Yes, sir," we all said in unison. We already knew what to do. Each one of us had a room that we knew we could clean up pretty well. Shirley took the kitchen; she was older and could reach the high cabinets. Carolyn took the bathroom; she could get that place clean in a heartbeat. And I got our room. I was the youngest, so I got the easiest job. I already knew where everything went, and I could make the bed by myself.

As we spread out to the different rooms, my father caught me by the arm. "Where do you think you're going?" he asked. "You come back here and clean this living room up."

Reluctantly, I turned around and grabbed an ashtray. I emptied it in a trashcan in the kitchen and brought it back. I bent over to pick up a toy, and suddenly I was on the ground. He kicked me right between the legs from the backside.

"Boy, you better hurry up!" He snarled.

I started to cry. It hurt so badly! Annoyed, my father then picked me up and started yelling, "You'd better shut up, or I'm going to beat your ass until you can't stand up!"

I tried to even out my breathing, scared of what he might do if I didn't calm down. But I just couldn't do it. The tears were still flowing down my face, and I could feel my cheeks getting hotter and hotter. I was fighting with everything within me to not cry, but it was just not working.

"That's it!" he yelled, shaking me. "March into your room, and put your clothes and toys in a box because I'm taking you to nigger town!"

My dad was *very* prejudice against blacks; he claimed two black men beat him with a rubber hose when he was a little kid.

I went to my room and packed my clothes and toys in a box, scared of what was going to happen to me. Three years old and I was about to be homeless. All I wanted to do that morning was watch cartoons. I should have known that in my house, your day could turn on a dime.

I carried my belongings to the living room, still in tears. "Why are you still crying, boy?" he said, taking a drag of a cigarette.

"Why do I have to leave?" I asked, my bottom lip quivering.

"I'm taking you to nigger town because you don't know how to mind!" he said. "*Those* people would just love to kill a little white boy who's running around in *their* neighborhood."

I fell to my knees. "Please, Daddy, don't make me go. *Please*!"

"Well, it's your own damn fault," he said. "If you could just learn to mind…but it's obvious you are a worthless, no-account piece of shit. So get your ass to the car, and load your stuff so we can go."

I tried so hard not to cry, but I just couldn't help it. I cried all the way out to the car, carrying my box. I loaded my stuff

1-800-4-A-CHILD
www.callingallhearts.com

inside the car and climbed in. I started sobbing, my whole body shaking. *I'm going to die*, I thought. *They're gonna kill me.*

I don't know how long I sat in the backseat before I fell asleep. But when I woke up, it was dark, and fear gripped my heart. I felt like someone was choking me. I stood up in the seat and looked around to see if anybody was near.

I could see lights on from the house and shadows moving around outside. The side door on the house popped open, and out walked my dad. My heart started to beat rapidly inside my chest. It was hard to breathe.

My dad was a very scary-looking man. Even though he was only about five foot seven, he weighed about 225 pounds, and he was as strong as an ox. He had tattoos running down both arms—some from when he was in the Korean War, and others were the names of his two kids from a previous marriage.

As he made his way to the car, fear gripped me even harder. My mind started running wild. *How am I going to survive in* that *part of town? I think it's dark, and maybe I can hide somewhere where no one will find me.*

Before I knew it, the back door of the car popped open, and I was grabbed by my hair. He jerked me out of the car and slammed me on the ground. I started bawling. He picked me up by the hair again and said, "Boy, you better quit that crying and learn to take your whippings like a man!"

I was fighting with desperation to stop crying, but it was so hard when the pain was so intense. He then asked me, "Do you think you can learn to be a good boy?"

"Yes!" I said immediately.

"When you address me, boy, you do it as yes *sir*."

I stuttered for a minute, trying to clear my throat and get out from under all that fear, and was finally able to squeeze out a tiny, "Yes, sir."

"What did you say?"

"Yes, sir!" I said louder.

"Well, that's more like it," he said, dropping me on the ground. "Grab your clothes and toys and put them back in the house."

It dawned on me about ten years later that I never heard my dad refer to our house as a *home*. He always said "our house" or "the house," never "our home." Looking back, it never really was a *home* anyway. It was just a place where I lived out the most degrading, terrifying years of my life.

I took my clothes and toys back in the house and put the box beside my bed. My sisters stared at me as I crawled into bed, sobbing, with tears covering my pillow until I fell asleep.

Yesterday

Why did no one hear my cry?
It seemed like I was
Destined to die.
Why couldn't they see it in my eyes?

1-800-4-A-CHILD
www.callingallhearts.com

Chapter Two

The next morning, I woke up thinking everything that happened the day before was all just a bad dream. Then, I realized it wasn't. I started to feel the pain from the day before.

The top of my head was throbbing from having my hair pulled twice. My bottom was still hurting from being kicked so hard. I tried to figure out in my mind what I did wrong, why he did that to me, and what I'd have to do to make sure it didn't happen again.

I sat up in bed for a moment, assessing my wounds and thinking over what I did to deserve it. *Was I really just a bad kid? Did I just not know how to mind? Was I always going to be like this? Was he always going to be like this? Would I turn out like him?*

It was a lot for a child to process.

"Get washed up!" I heard my mom call. "Breakfast!"

I got dressed and hurried downstairs for breakfast. It was eggs and toast, my favorite! Before I sat down, I looked around the kitchen. Dad was nowhere in sight.

"Momma," I said. "Where's Daddy?"

"He's gone to get his truck worked on," she said, sliding an egg onto my plate. "He'll be back after a while."

Maybe today will be better than yesterday, I thought.

"Momma, after breakfast, can I go outside and play?"

1-800-4-A-CHILD
www.callingallhearts.com

"Sure," she said. "But stay in the yard." My mother's tone was very flat.

I looked up at her face. Her eyes were downcast, and she looked upset. I started to worry. *Did I do something to make her upset?*

My stomach twisted inside of me, and I started to feel the pangs of guilt. What could I have done to make her sad?

My sisters finished eating before I did and headed off to their room to play. I finished up breakfast and went outside. I walked to the corner of our yard, hoping to catch Jerry Kimbell from across the street. I didn't want to be alone.

Jerry was my best buddy. Jerry and I had a lot in common. We were both full of energy and loved to play Cowboys and Indians, and our dads both drove trucks. We *loved* those big trucks.

As I waited by the fence, I saw no sign of Jerry anywhere, so I headed to the backyard, crawled inside the doghouse, and sat down. I went over the events of the past day.

My mind went crazy while I thought about what I must have done to make my dad so angry. I thought back and came to the conclusion that maybe I had just moved too slowly for my dad's liking. I decided that next time I'd be much faster.

But why didn't Shirley and Carolyn get into trouble? I was doing the same thing they were doing—cleaning the house! Maybe I was not as good at that as they were. I'd have to do better next time.

It was dark and quiet in the doghouse. I could think about things and not be disturbed. I started to feel safe in that dark, lonely corner by myself, so I stayed there for a long time.

1-800-4-A-CHILD
www.callingallhearts.com

When I heard the airbrakes set on the truck, I jumped. I wasn't sure that's what it was until I heard the air noise the truck made when it stopped. I wondered if I should just stay in the doghouse or get out. My preference was to stay in there because I felt safe. I decided to get out before my dad came looking for me. I ran out of the doghouse and around to the front yard just as he was climbing down off the truck.

He saw me and asked, "Are you being a good boy today?"

I replied just as I had been taught the previous day, "Yes, sir."

"You better have because I'm not going to put up with anybody who doesn't do what I say."

We went inside the house together, and I saw my mom waiting for him. She immediately started quizzing him as to why he was gone for so long.

"I was gone because I was gone, woman," my dad said.

"*Woman*?" my mother repeated incredulously.

They continued to argue for a while as I slipped out the side door and headed to the doghouse. I curled up in a little ball in the corner of the doghouse, waiting. I don't know how long I was in there, but the next thing I knew, I heard the side door of the house open and shut.

"Rodney! Rodney!" my mother called out. Before she was able to get to a third "Rodney," I was out of the doghouse and rounding the corner of the house.

"Where've you been?" she asked, hands on hips.

"Just out playing," I said.

1-800-4-A-CHILD
www.callingallhearts.com

"You'd better not be in those tall weeds out back! There's junk hidden in them weeds, and you could get hurt!" she scolded.

"Yes, ma'am, Mom," I said. "I won't go back there in them weeds at all."

"All right." She sighed. "You'd better get in the house. It's time for supper."

We sat down to mashed potatoes, gravy, corn, and fried chicken. I thought it was great. I *loved* fried chicken.

Everyone was filling his or her plates. I was distracted by my father's furrowed brow and squinted eyes. I knew better than to ask him what was wrong, so I dropped my gaze and spooned some potatoes onto my plate.

My dad asked me what I had been doing all day. I answered, "Just playing."

He pursed his lips and said, "Boy, don't you *ever* let me catch you messing with that dog or the doghouse. Because if I do, I will tear your ass up."

My mind ran rampant, trying to figure out how he knew. I didn't even see him at all that day! That is, until he got home. Did my sisters see me and tell? Did Mom?

My stomach started to hurt. I knew that I was in for it. I was still sore from yesterday's beating. I hoped he wouldn't break anything.

My hesitation made Dad angry. He slammed his fist on the table and said, "Boy, did you hear me?"

1-800-4-A-CHILD
www.callingallhearts.com

I immediately reply, "Yes, sir!" I struggled to finish my meal because of the inner pain. I was starting to feel sick. I pushed my plate away and stared at my food.

"You ain't getting up until you finish your food, boy," my dad said, rising from his chair. I pulled my plate back to me and started to eat. When my father was out of earshot, my mother said, "You can watch television when you're done, so hurry up."

I got the food down somehow because I liked to watch TV, especially cartoons. Unfortunately, there were no cartoons on because it was a Sunday night. After dinner, we all watched a show about cowboys and Indians until I was told to go to bed.

As I crawled into bed, I was so thankful that I survived the day without getting a beating. It bothered me that Daddy might have found out about my new hiding place. The dark, lonely corner of that doghouse was starting to become my only hope of survival. Tears welled up in my eyes, and I soon fell asleep.

But a Child

I am but a child,
Wanting to be loved,
Not kicked around
And pushed and shoved.

I need to run
And have lots of fun,
To be able to laugh,
And not be slapped.

I am a little one,
I'm not very tall,
So please, don't throw
Me against the wall.

I am but a child,
And I'm not always right,
But please don't hit me
When you feel like a fight.

I am but a child.
Now I'm gasping for breath,
Praying this beating
Won't be my death.

1-800-4-A-CHILD
www.callingallhearts.com

Chapter Three

The next week flew by. It always did when I knew Daddy would be out driving for an entire week. I couldn't wait for the days when my dad would be out on the road. I lived for those days.

Mom, my sisters, and I loaded up in the old Pontiac and headed downtown to do some shopping. I remember going into those stores seeing all that stuff and thinking, *Wow, if I could just stay here and play, I'd be happy for the rest of my life!*

There were toys in every store we went into. My mother could always find me gazing at the new toys. When I would ask for something, I was always told no because we didn't have the money to buy toys. All we could buy was food. As my mother put it, "You can't eat toys."

I never made a big deal about it because I didn't want to get scolded. I don't ever remember my sisters asking for toys, and I assume that they, at some point, had been told the same story.

After we piled back in the car, my mom turned the key. It wouldn't start. My mother was very angry. "I'm so sick and tired of telling your dad that we need another car!"

We sat there for what seemed like an eternity. Mom kept trying and trying to get it to start, but it just wouldn't budge. Finally, she said, "We'll just have to walk."

1-800-4-A-CHILD
www.callingallhearts.com

We started down the sidewalk in front of the stores with plate-glass windows. I could see my reflection in the monster-sized glass, and I thought I was a big boy.

As we neared the corner, Mother made a left turn, and we went halfway down the block to a barbershop where she grabbed me by the hand and took me through the door. The barber was an elderly gentleman, and he was cutting a man's hair. He paused when he saw my mother standing there and said, "Can I help you, ma'am?"

She said, "I'd like to leave my son here to get his hair cut." Then she proceeded to tell him how it was to be cut. She told him to cut it short but not all the way to the scalp and to please make it the same length all over. She told me to sit in one of the chairs and she would be back to get me later.

Then, in her best warning voice, she said, "Boy, whatever you do, make sure you stay in the barbershop until me and your sisters return. If you leave, I will make sure your dad finds out."

Knowing what that meant, I decided I would certainly stay put after my haircut. Shortly thereafter, I was up in the barber chair sitting on a board that went from one of the arms across to the other. It was brown, covered and had a little soft square seat right in the middle. As I was squirming to get comfortable, the barber was wrapping a sheet around me that covered my whole body and fastened at the back of my neck. He took his clippers and started cutting my hair. As the clippers ran across my head, I winced.

1-800-4-A-CHILD
www.callingallhearts.com

I thought maybe the barber was being a little rough with me because my mother was so particular about my haircut. Maybe he just didn't like kids? I tried to sit as still as I could, thinking if I cried, my dad would somehow find out.

By the time he had finished, my whole head was on fire. He helped me down out of the chair and sat me in one of the waiting chairs. I couldn't figure out what had just happened to me. I didn't look at the barber, for fear he might throw something my way or yell at me for looking at him. After what he just did to my head, I wouldn't have doubted it.

A few minutes later, my mom walked through the door. "What in the world happened to *you?*" she cried, seeing me in the chair.

The barber overheard her and said, "I cut his hair just like you told me."

My mom started yelling at the barber about what he had done. After a few moments of bickering, my mom finally paid him fifty cents for the haircut, and we left.

By that time, most of the burning had stopped. I tried to block out the arguing between my mother and the barber. I closed my eyes and started to think about how big I looked when I was sitting in that barber chair, gazing into that mirror. It sure was neat! I was almost as tall as the barber! I kept focusing on the chair and how fun it was—before my head caught on fire—to sit up there. I heard my mother stomp over to me, and I opened my eyes.

We headed out the door and started back down the street where the car was parked. Mother had me and my sisters wait on the sidewalk while she tried to start the car again. It sounded like it might start that time, but it didn't. It started that low, dragging, groaning sound that we had heard before.

Mother finally got out and said, "We'll just have to walk home." We all fell in behind Mother and started the mile-and-a-half trek home. It seemed like it took us forever. Not only because I was so young but because my sisters were taunting me about my haircut.

"Nice haircut, Rodney," Shirley said. "What, you get in a fight with a lawn mower?"

Carolyn giggled loudly and caught my mother's attention. "Leave him alone!" she called behind her. "Or I'll have the barber do the same to your hair!"

That shut them up.

As I watched my mother turn her face, I saw tears running down her cheeks. I wanted to ask her what was wrong, but I was afraid she might yell at me; I did not want that to happen today.

We finally reached home, and I could tell that my mother was still upset. I asked if I could play outside. She said yes but told me not to leave the yard. I went out to the corner of the fence to see if Jerry Kimbell was playing outside. I called for him, and he didn't respond.

I headed toward the doghouse and saw the old birddog lying on the ground. I didn't say anything to him or touch him at all. I slipped past him and crawled into the doghouse. I sat in the far, dark corner and thought. I remembered a week

1-800-4-A-CHILD
www.callingallhearts.com

earlier, the way my dad beat me and yelled at me. I kept wondering why that was happening to me and what I had done.

I rubbed my head with my hands because it felt so different from previous haircuts. It still had a little bit of a sting to it, and then I started to wonder if I somehow had made the barber mad. Why would he do something like this to me?

All of a sudden, I heard my oldest sister hollering at me. "Rodney! Rodney! Where are you?"

I crawled to the opening of the doghouse, pausing before I came out to make sure she didn't see me. When Shirley caught sight of me, she asked me where I'd been.

"On the other side of the house," I replied.

She eyed me skeptically. "Momma's got supper ready."

"Why haven't you been playing outside?" I asked.

"Me and sis have been helping Mother cook," she said, starting to walk back inside.

"What's for supper?"

"Meatloaf and vegetables."

After dinner, we watched some television and then laid down for bed. I had a hard time going to sleep that night. I was thinking about what might happen when my dad got home. With the car not working and me upsetting the barber, what was he going to do?

Maybe I'll get lucky and he will be in a good mood, I thought. Then I scolded myself for being so naïve. I knew that wasn't a possibility.

When I woke up, I realized it was Sunday. I heard Mother saying, "Get up! Get up! We're going to church!"

I bathed quickly, and Mother put my newest jeans on me with my new black boots. I was excited, hoping there would be someone there who would be kind to me. We started out the door, and I remembered our car was not there because it was still downtown. So we started walking to the church.

Bible Baptist Church was pastored by Brother Floyd. Most people knew him as Reverend Vernon Floyd. But once we were inside the church, he was known as Brother Floyd. He seemed like a giant to me. He had broad shoulders and dark, wavy hair. He always was very kind to me, patting me on the head when I walked past him.

I started to think about how my dad hated me and how I could tell Brother Floyd. I decided not to say anything to him at all, thinking he might tell my dad. The people at this church were so nice to my sisters and me that I could hardly believe it. Strangers I didn't even know were picking me up and hugging me and making me feel like I was special.

After leaving the church, we started our walk home. While going by the Kimbells' house, I saw my friend Jerry out in the front yard.

"Hey, Rodney!" he called from the fence. "Wanna come over and play?"

"Can I, Mother?" I asked.

"After you eat and change clothes you can."

"Jerry!" I hollered back. "I'll be over in a little while!"

We reached home, and we all went in to change clothes and my sisters started laughing about all the little old ladies that were picking me up in church. All the while I'd been thinking of how good it felt to get all those hugs. As we sat down to eat, my sisters asked my mother why all those old ladies at church kept picking me up.

"That's just what old ladies do," she said. "They like to pick up little kids and hold them." I told my mother they had been laughing at me because of it. She made no reply at all.

I finished eating quickly and asked if I could go to Jerry's to play. Mother said, "You better stay out of the street."

I took off out the door and hurried across the street to Jerry Kimbell's. He was waiting on me with two sticks. He had one for him and one for me. Those were to be our guns. Neither one of our families had enough money to buy us play guns, so we improvised by using sticks.

After chasing each other around his house for a while and shooting at each other, we decided to take a seat on their porch and pretended we were driving trucks. Both of our dads drove trucks, and we certainly enjoyed pretending we were truck drivers.

We had only been playing make-believe for a little while when Jerry's mom came out and told him he had to go inside for a nap. I felt devastated; I wanted to play! We were having so much fun; I did not want it to end.

I reluctantly headed back home, deciding not to go in the house but to head on out to my secret spot inside the doghouse. I sat there and started to reflect about church that morning and how good it had felt to be loved. Then, I started to wonder why my own dad was so mean to me. What had I done to make him so angry with me? It *must* have been me. I

1-800-4-A-CHILD
www.callingallhearts.com

tried to hold back the tears, but they started flowing until it seemed like there were no tears left.

Shortly thereafter, I heard my sisters yelling at me to come in and eat. After we ate, Mother put us to bed.

Please God

I'd like to have peace
If for only one night.
I just don't think
I can take another fight.

I pray to God,
Please, don't let him beat me again!
I am already wanting to die.
Please, oh God, I'm only ten.

Please God, just once in a while,
Could You give me a reason to smile?
Life for a child shouldn't be so tough
It seems like his life is roughing me up.

Please God, oh please, find me
Just one person to care,
Please God, oh please, just someone
To help me get out of here!

1-800-4-A-CHILD
www.callingallhearts.com

Chapter Four

The next morning after I woke up, I heard the sound of that big diesel truck pulling up in front of our house. I started to visualize how cool it looked and just how neat those air-brakes sounded.

Then, it dawned on me that my dad was home. I started sweating, and my heart pounded. My mind raced with all the possible things he might do to me this time. As I saw him walking through the door, Mother met him there and started to tell him about the problem with the car and how it was still in downtown Frederick. Then, I heard her call my name.

"Rodney, get in here right now!"

I went into the room, and she showed dad my head and burst out crying as she was telling the story. My dad looked at me and asked, "Why did you let that barber do that to you?"

"I don't know," I said as he gave me a disgusting look.

My father growled. "I'll take care of the car, Vida."

I watched him leave the room and go out the front door. He knocked on the Kimbells' front door. When Eugene, Jerry's dad, answered, they spoke for a moment, got into Eugene's car, and drove off. Later that day, he showed back up with the car.

My father came inside the house, hollering at my mother. "Where's the shotgun?"

"It's in the closet," she said. "What do you need it for?"

"Don't worry about it," he said gruffly, pushing past her. Then, he hollered for me. I panicked. *Was he going to kill me?* I watched as he grabbed the shotgun from the closet and walked out to the car. I followed close behind him, trembling with fear.

He put the shotgun in the back seat of the car and turned to me. "Boy, you'd better get in that car, *now*."

Not wanting to get hit, I ran as fast as I could to the car. I flung the door open and climbed in as quickly as possible. My father was right behind me. He threw the car into reverse and peeled out of the driveway."

"Boy," he said. "I had better not find out you had anything to do with that haircut, or I'm going to tear your ass up for hurting your mother." He then hit me across the chest. I was not expecting it, and it knocked the wind out of me. I lost my nerve, thinking I was going to die. I couldn't help but start crying.

"Look at you," he said. "You're acting like a *baby*." Unable to say anything—because I was gasping for air—I lay there, fear stricken. It felt like my eyes were going to pop out of my head.

I started to get my air back and tried breathing deep. I was just getting it under control when I realized what had just happened to me. I looked to my right and saw the shotgun. I was horrified. I struggled to not cry, but I couldn't hold back the tears. I started sobbing, and my father hit me again and told me to shut up.

1-800-4-A-CHILD
www.callingallhearts.com

After what seemed like an eternity, we pulled up in front of the barbershop. My dad turned the engine off and kept looking in the rearview mirror. I heard footsteps, and my father responded quickly. He popped open his door, jumped out, took out the shotgun, and grabbed me by the hand. He actually pulled me from the backseat through his driver's side door!

I looked around nervously, wondering what we could be doing here. Noting my father's anger and the shotgun, I immediately feared for the barber. I struggled to keep up with him as he moved swiftly across the street. My father slammed the barber shop door open, sending the bell on the door flying. It landed with a crash at the old barber's feet. He jumped when he heard the bell and turned to the door. His face went pale as he looked from me, to my father, and to the shotgun.

I was shaking all over as my dad dragged me nearer to the barber chair. He then turned me loose and started to give the barber a severe tongue lashing for the way he cut my hair.

"How stupid do you have to be to cut a boy's hair like that, huh?" my father demanded. "What's the matter with you, dumbass?"

Shaking, the barber exclaimed, "I cut his hair *exactly* the way *she* told me to cut it!"

My dad shoved the barrel of the shotgun right under the chin of the barber. I looked around for a place to hide. *If he shoots him*, I thought, *he may shoot me next!*

There was no place for me to hide, so I grasped the side of the barber chair and continued to shake uncontrollably.

1-800-4-A-CHILD
www.callingallhearts.com

"Old man," my father said, talking to the barber, "if you ever cut his hair like that again, I will come down here and blow your head off. Now, do you understand that?"

The old barber replied, "Yes, sir. It will never happen again, and you have my word on that."

My dad pulled the shotgun away from him and grabbed me by the hand. As we started out the door, my dad paused at the door for a minute as he turned around. "You understand me, old man?"

"Yes, sir," he replied. "Never again."

We headed home. I was relieved that my dad said nothing on the short journey back. When we got home, he put the gun in the closet and sent me off to bed. I tried to go to sleep, but I was still shaking all over thinking about what had happened. I started to cry and covered my head with the blanket, with the hopes that no one could hear me. I eventually fell asleep.

The next morning, I heard Dad's truck groan to a start, and I wondered what was up. I snuck into the living room and hid behind a chair.

"Vida," I heard my dad say, "I'm going to Texas. I should be home Friday night."

I heard footsteps and the front door open. "You'd better be home Friday night," my mother called after him.

I wish he'd never come back, I thought. I snuck out of the living room back to the bedroom and got dressed.

1-800-4-A-CHILD
www.callingallhearts.com

I found my mother and asked if I could go to Jerry's.

"They're not home," she said. "They've gone to their grandma's house and won't be back until next week."

I felt deflated. My morning started off well enough, what with Dad leaving for a week. But all hopes of getting to play were smashed. I tried to think who else might want to play, but I couldn't call anybody.

I went outside and scanned the neighborhood. The Jeffcoat boys lived next door, but it seemed they were not at home that day either. I looked around for something to do, and I saw a caterpillar crawling up the side of the house. I put a stick in front of him and watched him crawl onto the stick. I carried him around the yard until he dropped from the stick.

My only friend today just left me, I thought.

I wanted to disappear. The closest I could get to fading away was in my secret spot. I walked to the backyard and climbed back into the doghouse. Finally, I felt safe. But soon, bad thoughts started to seep in.

Why does my dad hate me so much? This thought was always in the back of my mind. I could never escape it.

I started to go over all the things about me that maybe my father didn't like about me. *I don't look like him*, I thought. *I have red hair and freckles. Is that what he doesn't like? Am I just so bad that I don't even know it?*

I wished that he would pick me up and hold me like those little old ladies had at church. It made me feel so good! Why couldn't he be like other dads and just tell me he loved me and play catch with me? Why did he have to hurt me so much?

1-800-4-A-CHILD
www.callingallhearts.com

I then decided I would have to start being good so he would not hurt me. I started thinking about all the things I could do in order to be a better boy.

Before I knew it, my dad was back, and it was Saturday morning. My sisters and I were up early, watching cartoons. I caught a glimpse of my dad going into the bathroom. I watched as he barely made it into the bathroom, turned, and walked into the living room.

He started pulling his belt off, and I froze with fear. "Who the *hell* didn't flush the toilet?"

I knew who came out of the bathroom last. It was my sister Carolyn. Nobody said anything. We were all fear-stricken statues. When nobody responded, I saw my father's nostrils flare and heard the belt start to fly.

The belt swooshed by my ear, catching Shirley's legs. When Dad swung again, he got my back and shoulder. Carolyn caught it against her arm and stomach.

The girls were crying, and I was just trying to endure the pain and not cry. When he hit me across the back again, it burned. I finally broke down and started to cry.

"If you don't stop this crying, I'll really let you have it!" my father roared. "You hear me?"

We all tried very hard not to cry, but our stinging limbs kept us from it. My dad began to whip me with the belt harder than before, and I begged him to quit.

"Please, Daddy," I pleaded. "Don't hit me again. Please! Oh, *please!*"

My begging went unnoticed while he whipped my sisters. Then, he sat us all down and said, "Somebody better tell me the truth, or this is gonna go on *all day*."

Finally, I spoke up. "It wasn't me. I haven't done that since you told me the last time not to do it. Please, please, don't hit me again."

He then threatened my sisters again that if they didn't tell him the truth, he was going to whip their asses again. They both cried out, "Rodney did it!"

I started screaming, "No, I didn't! Please, Daddy! You have to believe me. I'm telling you the truth. I didn't do it! Please don't hit me anymore!"

I was desperately hoping he was either going to believe me or decide I'd been beaten enough. I had no such luck. He sent my sisters to the bedroom.

"You little bastard," he seethed. "I've had it up to here with you lying to me!"

I crouched down low, like a dog about to be smacked with a newspaper.

"Turn over!" he said, spinning me around. He started whipping my back, rear end, and legs. I screamed out in desperation, hoping that someone would stop him. Nobody did.

My body started to go numb as he continued to beat me.

My tears began to dry, as I could feel nothing anymore. I could only lie there. He was yelling at me, but I couldn't hear what he was saying. My mind had somehow blocked out everything around me. He finally reached down and pulled me

1-800-4-A-CHILD
www.callingallhearts.com

up on the couch. I was still not saying anything. It was like my body had so much pain that it shut my brain off.

Maybe he is starting to see what he's doing to me, I hoped. *How could my sisters do this to me?*

I didn't understand until a few years later that they were just as scared witless as I was. They thought they were doing what they had to, just to survive.

My father left me sitting on the couch for a while with the TV on. I just kept staring at the floor in sort of a comatose state. He finally told me to "get my ass in bed."

I got up and headed straight for my room, not even turning my head to the side. I walked straight to the bed and climbed in. Somehow, I knew my life would always be like this. It didn't matter how hard I tried to please him; he'd still hate me.

I tried sleeping, but my eyes were wide open. I wasn't even blinking. I didn't know how I'd managed to finally get to sleep. I woke up later in the day, and I couldn't believe how much I was hurting. I was so sore, and I noticed the backs of my legs were black and blue. It terrified me to see all those marks.

I walked into the living room, and Dad said, "There's my little man." I looked behind me, expecting someone else to be there. *Surely he wasn't talking to me.*

"Come sit by me on the couch," he said. I climbed onto the couch and sat beside him. "Vida," he said, calling to my mother. "Fix Rodney somethin' to eat."

I sat there, stone-faced and stoic. "You *are* my little man, aren't you?" he asked me.

I said nothing. All I could think about was the lashing I just received at his hands. I didn't want to say anything; I was certain that whatever I did from that point on would be wrong.

"You want to watch something on television?" he asked.

"No, sir," I said. I started to feel that he might be feeling a little bad about beating me by the way he was acting. Even if that was the case, it didn't change me at all. I didn't care anymore. It didn't matter what happened to me.

Could this be some guilt finally rearing its head? I pondered. *Or is he just setting me up for the next big fall?*

He seemed to be trying to rid himself of the guilt he must have been feeling because he sat with me the rest of the day. When my mother brought me a sandwich, I barely took three bites.

I sat there next to him, staring at my feet, listening to the sounds of *I Love Lucy*.

Put through Hell

I was hit, I was kicked,
I slipped and fell,
I was told I could
Go straight to hell.

I was beaten to the point
I wanted to run.
Life for me as a child

1-800-4-A-CHILD
www.callingallhearts.com

Was never any fun.

I had no place to go,
And there was no hope for help.
He continued to beat me,
Sometimes using the barber strap for a belt.

Why did no one hear my cry?
It seemed like I was
Destined to die.
Why couldn't they see it in my eyes?

Why was I put on this earth
To go through this hell?
Oh, if there would have been
Just one person I could tell.

1-800-4-A-CHILD
www.callingallhearts.com

Chapter Five

The next morning was Sunday. I woke with a start, seeing my mother standing next to my bed, holding clothes.

"Here," she said, pulling a pair of jeans on me. "Put these on. Here's you a shirt, too."

"But, Momma," I said, pulling a long-sleeved shirt over my head. "It's warm outside."

My mother ignored me. "If you go outside, do *not* leave the yard. Don't be going to anyone's house. And…nobody can come over either."

I ate breakfast and then went outside, wondering why I had to wear these clothes, and why couldn't anyone come over to play? I sat down on the front steps to think.

Shirley walked up behind me. "They don't want anyone to see your bruises," she said as if reading my thoughts.

As she walked away, I wondered if Daddy was going to try and be nice to me again today. Surely he wouldn't hit me again…would he?

I jumped off the steps and walked toward the doghouse. I crawled inside and sat down. I started to wonder if this was normal and if other kids had this happen to them. Maybe I should ask them?

I leaned back farther into the corner and started to feel safe, like nobody could find me. I felt like I could disappear in there and no one would ever be able to touch me again.

1-800-4-A-CHILD
www.callingallhearts.com

I enjoyed those thoughts; it was the only protection I had. I knew of no other way to escape the situation. I just hoped and prayed that no one would ever find my hiding spot. It would be the end of my existence.

Just as I was falling into a secure daze of happiness, my father's voice snapped me back to reality.

"Rodney! Rodney! Where are you, boy?"

I ran to the door of the doghouse to see where he was. He was looking over toward the garage, so I ran out of the doghouse and up beside the house and turned around and ran like I was coming from the side of the house. Immediately he started talking in his loud voice.

"Boy! Where have you been?"

"I've been on the side of the house playing," I replied.

He asked, "Why didn't you come when I first hollered at you?"

I said, standing on trembling legs, "I didn't hear you."

He eyed me skeptically. "Come with me. It's time you learned how to be a man."

I fell in behind him as he walked through the weeds. We wound up at the gate of the chicken pen.

The stench of chicken poop and dirty animal permeated the air. As we entered the coop, I wondered what we were going to do in there. Dad walked toward some chickens, sitting in the corner of the pen. He grabbed one of the chickens by the head and spun it around. The next thing I knew, the chicken was flopping all over the ground with blood gushing out of its neck, and he was holding its head in his hand.

I felt my knees buckle underneath me, and I felt dizzy. I had never seen a chicken get killed before. I backed up to the fence, afraid I might be next. This just solidified the fear I had of my father.

Before I knew it, he had another chicken in his hands, shoving it in my face. "Take it by the neck," he instructed.

I grabbed its neck and tried to hold on tight, but that chicken kicked, pecked, and fluttered until she got free.

My dad kicked my leg and said, "Boy, you better hang on to that chicken or you'll be next."

I knew what that meant. He would try to break my head off. Grabbing another chicken, he again made me take it around the neck.

The chicken slipped out of my hand, and I immediately braced myself for the next blow. My dad picked me up and threw me out the gate. I hit the ground with a thud.

"Go tell your mother I need a pan!" he yelled.

I started in that direction with tears in my eyes. When I had reached the door, my mother was standing there and asked, "What's wrong with you?"

"Nothing," I said. "Dad wants a pan."

"What kind of pan?"

"I don't know," I replied.

She handed me a pan with a word of advice, "You better mind your dad."

I took the pan and headed toward the chicken pen. By that time there were four headless chickens in the middle of the pen. Dad threw two of them in the pan and said, "Take those to your mother and get another pan. You'd better hurry, or I'll beat your ass."

I scurried across the yard, trying not to drop the pan. I was getting sick at the thought of the chickens that were alive a little while ago and were now dead. I pictured my dad's hands closing around my throat, leaving me to run out of air.

I felt like I was going to fall and die. I struggled to make it to the door where Mother grabbed the pan and handed me another one. I slowly started walking back and tried to regain my composure.

He was standing at the gate with the other chickens in his hand. He grabbed the pan and put the chickens in it and took off for the house. I ran as hard as I could for the doghouse. As I was running, I hit the back corner. My heart was beating like it was going to explode. I was gasping for air. As I realized the comfort of my hiding spot, I began to relax some and gradually my heart and breathing felt normal again. I felt good that I was able to get to my hiding spot without Dad noticing where I went.

As I thought about what had just happened, the tears started to creep out. I felt so sorry for those poor little chickens, and I wondered how anyone could ring their necks like that and it not faze them. It seemed to bring my dad joy watching those chickens die—as well as watching me shake as I wondered about his next move.

I heard the side door of the house open. I peered out of the doghouse and saw my mother dumping feathers in the trashcan. As she turned to go back toward the house, I slipped back to my corner.

The same sad, burdening thoughts crowded my mind as I tried to relax. I wished I could stay in the doghouse forever. I let my mind loose, wondering why my *whole* family didn't care for me.

I think that it must be because I'm a boy.

I just didn't know what was wrong with me. Why was I always getting beat up? I tried so hard to be good! It didn't seem to matter what I did. I was always wrong.

"Rodney!" I heard my sisters call.

I was very cautious so they wouldn't see me. I couldn't see them, so I shot out the door. As I was going around the corner of the house, they hollered that it was time to eat.

I sat down to eat, and I noticed we were having fried chicken. It was hard for me to eat having seen those poor chickens lose their heads in the chicken yard. I tried hard to eat it though. I knew that tomorrow would bring a sort of solace; Daddy would be gone for a week driving his truck, and I'd get some peace.

By the time my dad got back into town again, the soreness from my beating was pretty much gone, but there were still traces of bruises. Mom kept making me wear warm clothes to cover them up.

That Saturday morning, Daddy had me go outside with him to his truck. He still had a huge trailer behind it. It was so big, bright, and shiny that I somehow faded away in the beauty of it. I was totally awe stricken by its mirror-like finish.

He opened the back doors and climbed inside. There were boxes everywhere. He grabbed two and placed them on the ground. He closed the door and handed me a box, and we started inside.

Once in the house, he opened the boxes and pulled out small boxes of raisins. He opened one and gave it to me. They were so good! This started a long tradition of us getting raisins every week. We soon grew sick of them. I can't eat them anymore, even to this day.

After the raisin eating, he loaded me in the car. We pulled out of the drive and headed down the road. The gravel road was noisy as the tires picked up rocks and threw them at the bottom of the car at a rapid rate.

I imagined that the rock sounds were someone was shooting at us. I decided to say this, to see if it was going to be a good day or a bad day.

"Sounds like someone is shooting at us, Dad," I said, smiling at my imagination.

"Its just rocks, stupid."

Looks like it's going to be a bad day, I thought. I sat there and tried not to make a sound as we turned from the gravel road onto a brick street. The bricks made the tires sound like they were singing to us, but I decided not to say anything that time so I wouldn't get called stupid again.

We then turned on to a regular paved street and ended up at the hardware store. As we walked in, I saw a little pedal tractor in the window and an "Ooh" slipped out of my mouth.

Dad heard and grabbed me by the shoulder. "Boy, you'd better not open your mouth while we are in this store, or I'll beat your ass when we get home."

"Yes, sir," I said as he pushed the glass door open and entered the store.

Only Four

I was only four
When he walked in the door,
Looking to beat me
And seriously mistreat me.

Why he hated me
I'll never know.
If he loved me,
It never did show.

How could someone
So strong and so wild
Give that kind of beating
To such a small child?

Are they totally in
Utter despair,
Or is it the fact

1-800-4-A-CHILD
www.callingallhearts.com

They just don't care?

How does a person beat
Something so small and so weak,
Forcing them to always
Turn the other cheek?

How could you force them
To endure such pain?
Is it because your actions
You don't have to explain?

1-800-4-A-CHILD
www.callingallhearts.com

Chapter Six

I'm not exactly sure how soon after that Dad decided to quit driving a truck. All I really remember is how sad I was at the thought that I wouldn't see his shiny cab anymore. I really thought that truck was something.

I was also disappointed because this meant Dad would be home more often—something I did not want. I remember when he told us that he had quit and we were moving. I wasn't worried about moving so much as I was that I'd be even more likely to get beat every day.

I was devastated when I found out we were leaving Frederick. We'd only be about eleven miles from Frederick, in the little town of Hollister. But still, eleven miles was a big gap between a kid and his only friends.

So in the summer of 1959, we packed up and left for our new town. Hollister was a small little town with three grain elevators bordering the town on the north and a railroad running just north of the elevators. The town was seven blocks long and five blocks wide. Population was only about 120 people. My dad had a brother living there at the time and went to work for him doing plumbing jobs.

Our house was moved to Hollister from the country onto a vacant lot. Because of that, there was a tremendous amount of work to be done. And who got to do it? Me and my sisters, of course.

1-800-4-A-CHILD
www.callingallhearts.com

I hated working out in the lot. My dad had told us to rake up any weeds or leaves, clean up the lot of any garbage, and make it look tidy. That was a tall order for kids ranging in age from five to seven.

One afternoon, we were working on the west side of the house when we came across a large snake. I screamed, "Ah! Look out! A snake!"

Shirley gasped. "It's at least six feet long!"

"Run!" cried Carolyn. We all threw down our rakes and ran inside the house.

When my dad came home and found us hiding inside, he was fit to be tied. "Why aren't y'all in the yard working like I told you to?"

"Daddy," Shirley said, "there was a snake outside. It was bigger than us! We got scared."

"Bunch of dumbasses, I swear!" he yelled. "Why didn't you just go to another part of the yard and work?"

"We were scared, Daddy," I choked out, knowing what was going to happen next.

He gritted his teeth together and growled. "Line up!" he said.

I knew what that meant. My sisters and I all turned around, with our backs to my dad. I closed my eyes and braced myself for the blow. I heard the jingle of his belt coming loose. Then I heard a loud *thwack* as he started with Shirley. As soon as he busted her bottom, she ran off crying.

Then my other sister got it and did the same. My turn came up, and I was shaking.

"Bend over."

I bent over in front of the sofa and grabbed a cushion. The first few blows stung like crazy, and I thought he might be done. But that would've been too kind of my father. He just caught a second wind of fury and tore into me. I couldn't take any more. I fell to the floor.

"Get up!" he yelled. "And shut that blubbering up!"

I didn't even know I had started crying. I was too focused on the pain and fear that I had forgotten to try to control my tears. My crying just egged him on. Finally, as my dad started to wear out, I got up and ran to my bedroom. I shut the door quickly behind me. Thank God, he didn't pursue me.

After that, I had hoped that my dad would go easy on us for a day or two. In the past, I noticed he would beat the fire out of us and then leave us alone for at least a day. But that's when he was driving a truck and gone. Now that we were in Hollister, there was no such reprieve from him.

The very next day when Dad got home from work, he called all us kids into the house. "I've decided that you are going to get *three* whippings a day whether you need it or not."

My heart sank. That's when I realized it didn't matter what I did; I was going to get beaten.

Between working in the lot, hiding from my dad, and getting beaten three times a day, my life in Hollister was shaping up to be yet another hell. For a long while, I hadn't met any-

1-800-4-A-CHILD
www.callingallhearts.com

one my own age. Thankfully, though, one Sunday afternoon I met two boys about the same age as me.

They were just passing by our house when one of them called out to me.

"Hey!" the boy called. "What's your name? You new?"

"Yeah," I hollered back. "My name's Rodney."

"I'm Harry, and this here's Francis," said the boy named Harry, pointing to the other boy. "We're headin' down to the pond. Wanna come?"

"Okay!" I said, running to catch up.

As we walked, we talked. I told them about moving from Frederick and how my dad used to drive a truck. I was careful not to reveal too much though. When we reached the pond, Harry said, "This is it. We call it the Gin Tank, on account of the cotton gin over there."

I looked out onto the water. There was an old rickety pier, about fifteen feet long and two feet wide. It had a busted board on the right side and looked a little foreboding.

"Be careful over there," Francis said, pointing to the pier. "Momma says it's not very safe."

"Eh, I'm not scared," I said, trying to show off. I ventured out onto the pier, hoping to earn some respect from my new friends. There was an angle iron holding the boards up from the ground under the water. They stuck up past the boards about three feet. The boards had been painted blue but were really in bad shape. The anchor posts' paint had worn off; all of them were white.

1-800-4-A-CHILD
www.callingallhearts.com

I went out to the last anchor post on the left and started twirling around on the anchor post. I'd go off the pier over the water and back onto the pier.

"Woo!" I hollered, showing Harry and Francis that I was having a good time. They smiled and started to come a little closer.

As I swung, I noticed two older boys on the opposite side of the water fishing. They looked over at me, nodded their heads to say hello, and went back to watching their lines. I was just about to wave to them when my hands slipped, and I fell into the water.

For anyone else, this wouldn't be a problem. But I did not know how to swim. I started panicking. As soon as I went under the water, I couldn't breathe. I was fighting to get up out of the water. When I finally resurfaced, trying to get my breath, I screamed at the top of my lungs, "*Help! Help! Help!*"

All of a sudden, I felt someone grab my arm and pull me out of the water. I was gasping for air and trying to spit out water at the same time.

"You all right?" the boy said. It was one of the kids from the other side of the pond.

"Yes," I said, suddenly bursting into tears. The boy just patted me on the head, walked to the other side of the pond, and went back to fishing. I looked around to find that Harry and Francis had left.

God bless that boy, I thought. I didn't realize it then, but he was the first of three angels I'd come across in my life.

1-800-4-A-CHILD
www.callingallhearts.com

I went over by the old cotton gin, sat down, and cried. I was so scared; I knew if I went home I would get beaten. I knew I had to come up with a story or I was doomed. Suddenly, I had an idea.

I remembered it had rained and the ditches in front of the house were full of water. I decided I'd tell Momma and Daddy that's where I fell in and got wet. When I got home and told them my story, Dad jerked me by the arm. He dragged me into the living room, pulled off his belt, and whipped me with it.

It's True

Under our house
Was where I learned to hide.
I would start shaking all over
When I heard him come outside.

I was always in trouble,
No matter what I did,
And he always knew
Where I ran and hid.

He told me when I was five
I would get three whippings a day,
Whether I needed them or not,
And I could not go out and play.

1-800-4-A-CHILD
www.callingallhearts.com

My mom and dad always
Blamed everything on me.
I finally left home
When he beat me until I couldn't see.

1-800-4-A-CHILD
www.callingallhearts.com

Chapter Seven

The only good thing about Hollister was that I was old enough to start school. Even though I was always in trouble, I didn't mind it as much. The paddlings at school were *nothing* compared to what I got at home. Don't get me wrong; I made good grades; it was just so hard for me to concentrate. School was my reprieve. It was my sanctuary a few hours a day. I couldn't help but think about what I was going to have to go home to, even when the school day had just begun.

I remember watching kids get on the school buses to go home. We walked since we only lived two blocks away. My sisters and I would usually get one block east of the school and stop and watch the buses go by. I liked watching them go by. I had never ridden on a bus before, so I was always jealous of those who got to.

One day while watching the buses, I got the idea to let the school bus run over my foot. I figured if it hurt, it couldn't be any worse than what I got at home. I'm still not sure where that thought came from. Maybe I was starting to become fearless of pain since I had so much experience with it so far in my short life. Whatever reason, though, I wanted to see what it felt like to have the bus run over my foot.

As we watched the buses go by, I ran up to the front tire and stuck my foot under the tire, letting it run over my foot. To my surprise, it didn't hurt at all. So when the next bus

1-800-4-A-CHILD
www.callingallhearts.com

came by, I did the same thing. Again, no pain. I let the third one do it also. This went on for three days.

On the fourth day when I let the first bus run over my foot, it stopped. The driver came flying off the bus and started yelling at me.

"Kid, what is the matter with you?" he screamed, pointing a finger in my face. "I'm going to tell the superintendent!"

The next day, the superintendent came to my classroom. When the teacher asked him what she could do for him, he pointed at me. I gulped loudly. The superintendent told me to come with him. I was so scared.

He took me to the principal's office, went to a closet, and started pulling out wooden paddles. He pulled out three different paddles from a drawer, each one bigger than the other.

He whispered low, "These paddles *hurt*," he said. "Just look at the size of 'em."

He set them all out on the principal's desk. As I watched him, I could hardly talk. Those paddles were a lot bigger and a lot heavier than my daddy's belt. I knew they'd hurt.

The superintendent sat down and stared straight into my eyes. "See this one right here?" he asked, pointing to the biggest paddle. "I'm going to use it on you if you let *one more* school bus run over your foot. Do you understand me, young man?"

"Yes, sir," I replied quickly. "It'll never happen again."

And it never did. After I left the office, I was trembling with fear. Not because of what I just experienced but because of what I was afraid I was going to experience next.

Oh, no. I thought. *What if someone tells Mom or Dad?*

I prayed and prayed that they wouldn't find out. Thank the Lord they didn't!

I tried to stay out of trouble and far from my dad after the bus incident. I just wanted to "keep my nose clean" and steer clear of any problems. Of course, living in the house I did, I never really got that chance.

One night, after dark, I remember my dad coming home drunk. I heard him crashing around in the kitchen, dropping things, and muttering slurred curse words under his breath. When he started making threats to hurt my mom, she came into our room.

"Kids," she whispered. "Kids, wake up. I need you to put shoes on quickly and wait for me to come get you."

"Why, Momma?" Shirley asked.

"Girl, don't ask me why. Just do it," my mother replied hastily. She lowered her head and sighed. "Just…just be quick and *be quiet.*"

We put our shoes on fast and waited for Mom. I heard my mother sneak into the TV room and call my dad's sister, Wanda. She only lived about six hundred yards from us, across the street and over by the highway.

She whispered fast and low into the receiver.

"Vida!" my dad growled from the kitchen. "Where's those damn biscuits, woman?"

I heard her hang up the phone, and she soon appeared at our door. She put her index finger to her lips and went to let Wanda in the house. I heard Aunt Wanda talking to my dad.

Mom came back and snuck me and my sisters out the front door. I then heard what sounded like dishes breaking, and we ran faster. We made it over to Wanda's house and hid in one of her bedrooms. Momma went to the front door to let Wanda in when she heard footsteps.

"Better lock it, Vida," my aunt said as she leaped inside. "He's really in rare form tonight."

All four of us were extremely scared; we spent the night in Wanda's house. The next morning we went home to get ready for school, and there was a very scary sight. Dishes were scattered in little bitty pieces all over the kitchen floor. There was not *one* dish left intact.

"It's like a tornado," I whispered.

I heard my mom sniffle. I looked up and saw her eyes filling with tears. "Go get ready," she said quietly.

"Momma?" I reached out to her.

"I said, 'go get ready'!" she snapped. "You're gonna be late for school."

As my sisters and I walked to school, I wondered how a person could do that. When we got home from school, my mom and dad had cleaned up the mess. I remember seeing two big washtubs full of broken dishes. We had no money to buy more dishes, so we went to the grocery store in Frederick and bought tin pie plates and a bunch of plastic silverware. We had to use these over and over for about the next year.

Don't

I was his punching bag.
But he used no gloves.
All I ever wanted
Was just to be loved.

I wanted to be loved,
But I was truly hated.
If they made a movie of my life,
Because of the violence, it would be "R" rated.

When I would get up,
He would knock me back down.
I don't know why he didn't
Stick my head under water and watch me drown.

If you were beaten
When you were a just a kid,
Love your kids
And don't do what he did.

1-800-4-A-CHILD
www.callingallhearts.com

Chapter Eight

As it turned out, my family wasn't the most dramatic cluster of people in Hollister. Stranger things started to happen in our little town. There was a kid named Jesse Blair who went to school with me. He was a grade ahead of me and came from a rough family. I'm talking pistol-shooting, curse-word-spilling, face-punching type of rough. For whatever reason, Jesse liked to start trouble.

Another boy, Terry Bradley, was in my grade. He wasn't a bad kid; he lived out in the country and was really quiet. One winter afternoon, Terry went down to a pond near his house. All he did was stop to look at the ice when he heard a shot ring out.

Across the way, Jesse had walked up with a .22 rifle. He started shooting at the ice. Two bullets ricocheted off the pond and hit Terry in the hand and arm. Terry was rushed to the hospital where he was found not to have serious wounds. The sheriff of Tillman County came out to talk to Jesse. No one really knew what Sheriff Frank Kilgore told him, though. I'm sure it wasn't much. After all, the sheriff was his uncle.

In the spring of that year, there was a man named Hunk Rich who ran the post office. Hunk didn't do much around town except sit at the post office and drink. About three o'clock in the morning one night, Hunk went to visit Jesse's dad, Frank Blair. The two of them got pretty drunk and were joined by an old moonshiner, Slick Flemming.

Slick and Frank got into an argument with Hunk. At first, they just yelled and cussed at each other. Soon, however, it escalated into something worse. Slick pulled out a knife and passed it between he and Frank. Together, they stabbed Hunk Rich *twenty-five times*!

When they realized what they had done, they loaded Hunk in the back of Slick Flemming's 1961 Ford pickup. Slick drove him to the emergency room at Frederick Memorial Hospital, eleven miles away.

They took Hunk into the hospital where he died within two hours of multiple stab wounds. Slick Flemming was taken off to jail. The next morning, the news spread quickly.

Frank Blair was not arrested; he *was* the sheriff's brother-in-law. When I heard the news, I was terrified. Slick Flemming had been to our house many times, drinking with my dad. I thought if he got out of jail he might come to our house and shoot me because my dad had always told him that I was a worthless piece of shit. This situation caused my fear to multiply.

I don't know if it was because of all the commotion going on in town or my own fears, but I started waking up early in the mornings. Down the street there was a boy about my age named Melvin Matthews. He and I had become friends at school, and we would even walk home together.

1-800-4-A-CHILD
www.callingallhearts.com

One morning after I had woken up early, I got up, grabbed my fishing pole, and tapped on Melvin's window. He'd come with me and we'd walk to the Gin Tank.

When we came back from fishing one day, we were late for school. I didn't know what to do with my fishing gear, so I stashed it at Melvin's house. After school, I made a beeline to Melvin's house. I knew if I didn't get it home and back in its proper place, my dad would find out and beat me.

I searched where I had hid the pole but couldn't find it anywhere. I found Melvin and said, "I *have* to find my fishing pole, Melvin, or my dad will kill me!"

Melvin didn't say anything to me. He just stood there. I had a feeling Melvin knew where it was and just wasn't telling me.

"Melvin, tell me where it is!" I pleaded.

Silence.

I started crying. I knew what would happen if Dad found out what happened. About that time, Melvin's uncle came outside. "Sir, do you know what happened to my fishing pole?"

His uncle finally brought it out, busted into many pieces. My heart sunk to my stomach. I gathered up the sad remains of my pole and went home crying, every step of the way.

What am I going to do now? I thought. *He's going to kill me.*

I looked around for a place to hide my broken rod. I decided to hide it on the enclosed porch of our house. After that, I breathed a sigh of relief. Days passed, and nothing was said about the pole, and nobody had found it. I thought I was home free.

About three weeks later, my dad woke us kids up one Sunday morning and told us that we were going to clean off the porch. My heart sank. I hoped and prayed that he didn't find my fishing pole.

I tried to clean the area where the pole was hidden, but Dad pushed me aside, telling me I wasn't cleaning right. And then, it happened. My dad reached behind an old stool and pulled out the pieces to my fishing pole.

"Boy," he growled, "what the hell's this?"

"I don't know, sir," I stammered. I thought ignorance would be the card to play. Maybe if I played dumb, he wouldn't hit me. Or at least not hit me as hard.

"That's a bold-face lie, boy!" he yelled.

"No, Daddy, really," I said, putting my hands up to cover my face. "I really don't know!"

He grabbed a second piece of the rod and hit me across the face. I started screaming and crying. My mom and sisters watched, too gripped with fear to do anything.

I tried as hard as I possibly could not to cry. Daddy always told me he would beat me until I stopped crying. The pole left stinging, painful whelps all over my body. He kept screaming at me, "Who did this? Who did this, you little bastard?"

I couldn't tell him the truth, or I would be in even *more* trouble. I finally broke down and told him that it was me. That beating with the pole was the worst pain I had felt to date. The stinging was about to make me crazy.

About two weeks after that, I went to Melvin's house to try to find out why his uncle would do that to my fishing pole.

"I don't get it, Melvin," I said. "I thought you were my friend."

"My uncle just really hates your dad," Melvin said. "And I hate you."

I couldn't take it anymore. I was tired of it—tired of my dad, tired of not having any real friends, and tired of that stupid town. Before I knew what was happening, I balled up my fists and socked Melvin in the jaw. He went down with a thud.

I heard the front door open, and out came Melvin's momma, belt in hand. I was scared she was going to hit me, but then I heard her yell, "Get up and fight him, Melvin!"

He didn't move. She slapped him across the face with the belt. "Get up, boy!" she hollered at him. "Get up and fight him!"

Melvin got up, and I knocked him down again. Then, his mother started hitting him across the back with a belt. "I'm going to beat you until you whip him!" she cried.

Melvin tried to get up again, and I knocked him back to the ground. Melvin's mom kept lashing at him with her belt.

"Stop it!" I yelled at her. "Stop it! He ain't gonna be able to whip me!"

I turned on my heels and walked back to the house.

When I walked in, my mother was fixing dinner and told me to sit down at the table. I sat with my back to the back door, opposite my dad's spot. I heard my dad drive up, and my body started tensing up all over. My dad came in through the back door. He grabbed the back of my head, taking a chunk of hair, and slammed my face to the table.

To this day I can't sit with my back to the door.

That night, while lying in bed, I told God, "I can't take this anymore! I can't!"

I couldn't sleep. I kept reliving the events of the day: Melvin, his momma, and my dad. I kept seeing the belt flying and felt the pain in the back of my head, the tense feeling in my back and shoulders. Finally, I had had enough.

In the middle of the night, I snuck in to my mom and dad's bedroom. Off in the corner was a door to a great big closet. I slipped in, shut the door, and turned the light on, hoping and praying that he didn't hear me.

I walked over to the corner where there was a .22 rifle, loaded. I picked it up, walked back to the door, turned the light off, and snuck around the bed. I stood over my father with the gun in my hand, ready to fire. I was scared out of my mind.

I'll shoot him in the face and kill him, I thought. *You'll go to prison*, my mind told me.

I did *not* want to go to prison. Defeated, I went back to the closet and put up the gun. I went back to my bedroom, crying to God.

I can't take anymore!

In the midst of my tears and anguish, I somehow managed to fall asleep.

1-800-4-A-CHILD
www.callingallhearts.com

Darkness and Depression

Darkness is where I would go
When I needed to hide.
It's the place where depression
Was born deep down inside.

It grabbed me by the throat
And took me way down deep within.
I thought it was where I could live.
I was so deceived when I woke up.
I had to learn to forgive.

It finally dawned on me
It only showed up when I had bad thoughts,
So therefore I had
To put my mind on daily watch.

1-800-4-A-CHILD
www.callingallhearts.com

Chapter Nine

One day, my dad announced he was going to quit plumbing for his brother. He had gotten a job at Century Granite, back in Frederick.

Dad's new job at Century Granite was in the middle of an industrial park, full of other businesses. Because money was getting tight, my mother decided to go back to work. She found a job in the industrial park at a factory called Betsy Bra.

One day my sisters and I didn't have school, and my mom and dad rode to work together, leaving one car at home. It was a 1957 Chevy station wagon. My sisters and I were playing outside when Carolyn said, "I wish I could drive."

That's when I got the idea that *I* could drive. I ran inside, found the keys to the station wagon, and went out to start it. I could barely see over the dash. It had a three-speed manual transmission. I thought I knew how to operate it; I'd seen Mom drive it many times.

I knew that the way to start it was by pushing in on the clutch. It was already in low gear. I hit the gas, took off, and it started jerking. I gave it more gas, and it quit jerking. I went around the block and came in our circle drive.

Shirley, my oldest sister, was standing in the drive when I pulled up. "I want to ride on the hood, Rodney!" I pointed for her to get on. She climbed onto the fender and hoisted herself up to the hood.

I hit the gas and watched her face go from smiling to crying in an instant. She turned over on her stomach in the middle of the hood, hanging on only by the small lip between the hood and the windshield. I started swerving and eventually threw her off the car. I watched as she fell beside the road.

Panicking, I drove off and left her there. I went home, parked the car, and put the keys back where I found them. When I saw Shirley walking up the driveway, I ran out to her.

"Shirley, please don't tell Daddy!" I begged. "Please, please!"

As soon as my parents came home, she ran to the door and told them. My dad ran back to my room, grabbed me by the hair, and threw me down on the ground. I tried to get up, but he knocked me back down. All the while he was screaming, "Don't you *ever* drive that car again, you little bastard!"

My face felt like it'd been hit with a hammer, and there was blood everywhere. That's when my parents started taking the car keys with them whenever they left the house.

From then on, I started looking for ways to get out of the house and away from my dad. There was a farmer named Roy Grant who lived on the north side of town. I'd see him every now and then at the gas station and grocery store. He was always really nice.

One of our neighbors, Bobby Smith, worked for Roy. I'd always ask Roy if I could work for him whenever I saw him. He asked me how old I was and I told him.

"You're almost there," he said.

"Bobby isn't too much older than me," I'd argue. "And I'll work just as hard if not harder than him. I promise." Every night, I would pray that I could work for Roy. I just needed a way out of my house.

A few short months later, Roy saw me in town and told me he needed help that next Saturday. He said Bobby had lost control of one of his tractors and jumped off. He busted open his head and had to be stitched up, leaving Roy shorthanded.

My dad was out of town, so I couldn't ask him if I could go. He had gone hunting in the Wichita Mountains for coyotes with some people he knew. Mom said it was all right, and I was at Roy's house at eight o'clock in the morning that Saturday, anxious to get to drive a tractor.

Mr. Grant showed me how to drive the tractor. I was very nervous, always afraid I was going to screw up and someone would beat me. That fear made it hard for me to do anything at all.

I got on the tractor, and Mr. Grant followed me down to the highway. He told me that he would pass me and show me where to turn. It was a successful trip, and I relaxed just a little bit. We went back to his house and took another tractor to the same field. Mr. Grant was very patient with me and seemed to like me. I felt good around him.

That night, I went home feeling pretty good about myself. It had been a very long time since someone had been that kind to me. When I got home, my dad tore into me. I don't know why; he just did. I was stressed more than you could imagine.

I went to bed that night crying from more pain from yet another beating. I would beg God to help me; I knew

1-800-4-A-CHILD
www.callingallhearts.com

He could hear me. The next morning, Roy Grant called and asked my dad if I could help him. Thankfully, my dad said yes.

Because of Mr. Grant's kindness, I was able to get away from the beatings and mentally regroup before having to go on. I know that Roy Grant was really an angel, disguised as a farmer. Every night, I'd beg God for a way to get me out of the house. The next morning, Mr. Grant would call, asking for my help on his farm. I wouldn't have survived my childhood if it hadn't been for him. Working in his fields always gave me the break I needed to get away for a while. I needed as many breaks as I could get.

My dad was putting a water pump on an old GMC truck one evening and hollered for me to come help him. He made me get up on the front bumper and reach in for the water pump, holding it steady. I was so short; I could barely hang on to the pump.

"Hold it steady, dumbass!" he yelled. "Line the bolts up!"

It was dark, and I couldn't see anything. Suddenly, I felt the hair on the back of my head get pulled and felt my face meet something hard. My dad pulled my head up and slammed it down on the top of the motor. I felt blood flowing like a faucet on my forehead. My head had been busted open!

My dad backhanded me and knocked me on the ground, sending all the air in my lungs whooshing out. I lay on the ground until I could breathe again.

"Vida!" my dad called. "Vida!"

1-800-4-A-CHILD
www.callingallhearts.com

"What?" she asked, coming outside. I guess that's when she saw me because I heard her stifle a scream. "What happened?"

"Pick his dumbass up and take him to the hospital," my dad replied.

My mother ran inside, grabbed a washcloth, and had me put pressure on the bleeding. She walked me over to the car, and we both got in.

"Don't say anything at the hospital," she said, not looking at me. "When we get to the hospital, I'll do the talking. You hear me?"

I nodded, still a little unsure of where I was.

"If anybody asks you what happened, you tell them you fell on the concrete porch."

I didn't say a word all the way to the hospital. When we got to the hospital, I was rushed to the emergency room. The doctors and nurses started sewing my head up.

"What happened?" the doctor asked, looking at my mother intently.

"He's a clumsy kid," she replied. "He was foolin' around and fell off the concrete porch."

I started to cry. I realized there was no hope. There was no way I was ever going to get out of that hell, that torture I was living in.

"I'm sorry," the nurse said. "That probably hurts, huh?" She backed up a bit and let me have some space before she started sewing me up again.

I left the hospital with a broken heart and thirty-two stitches in my head.

Being Within

A tidal wave of emotions
Sometimes runs through my soul.
It's almost like falling
In a deep, dark, black hole.

I surface for air,
Searching through my thoughts.
Trying to grab hold of why
I'm always tied in knots.

I walk within myself
Searching for my inner being.
When I realize that it is a peace
That I'm finally feeling.

I know now that it is peace
That always comes from within,
And it has the power
To destroy all my sin.

1-800-4-A-CHILD
www.callingallhearts.com

Chapter Ten

The beatings were now more frequent and more aggressive. The pain was absolutely unbearable. I honestly believed I was going crazy. Every night, I begged God to help me.

I remember walking through the house one day thinking that I could tell I was about to lose absolute and total control of everything—physically as well as mentally. I knew beyond a shadow of a doubt that I was starting to go crazy. I just couldn't let it take me over. Although it would be easier than just dealing with my life.

Then, later that day it happened. I was sitting outside, and all the anger, rage, and fury started coming to me. What could I do to control something, *anything* in my world? I couldn't fight back with my fists, but I *could* fight back with my mind.

Thoughts crept into my mind of how to change the alphabet around and make my own language. I started to change letters to take the place of others. I swapped B for D; C for T.

When a part of a word sounded like an S or K, it was now a G. I changed H for W; J for P; S for T; T for S; V for F; W for H; Y for H because it sounds like a W; and no swap for I. So, if I were to see "forty-four," it would be changed to "volsy voul." Fifteen hundred would become "vivseem wumbleb." Sounds crazy but this language was there when I thought I was losing my mind. This *kept me* from going crazy. When

I got under torment and stress, I would start using this language over and over. It was a useful distraction.

Now that I had gotten older, and a little angrier, I started getting into a lot of fights. Once that started, it was *constant*. Every kid that my dad kicked the father's butt, I had to fight. I really didn't want to fight all the time, but people didn't give me a choice.

The problem was that I was not going to let anybody else beat on me. I became extremely aggressive and became determined to give back what I'd been getting. I quickly lost any fear of fighting or pain. I knew I was becoming a dangerous person. The fights were numerous because of my frustration and anger. I was not losing any fights.

It got so bad that I was taking on two to three kids at once. They could not win; I was ready to beat somebody myself. My heart was hurting because I didn't want to hurt anybody but felt like I had no choice. They came at me. I needed a way to get out my anger. It was just too perfect.

During this time, my dad became a "junker." He'd bring in old cars to get different kinds of metal off and sell for scrap. He had me help him every time. We did this a lot during the summers. We'd use the money to buy clothes for the next school year.

My dad would buy terribly old cars; they usually weren't running. We would take a tow bar, put it on the front of them, and pull them home. One Saturday my dad pulled the tow bar out of the shed and told me to start taking bolts out while he went to the station to get gas.

As I started to disassemble the hitch, I felt a devastating sting on the end of my finger. I couldn't believe how much it hurt! I kept on taking the bolts out, and it happened again. The hurting was so severe this time that I looked down and saw a scorpion digging into my skin.

My heart sank, and I gasped for air. I thought I was going to die. I had always been told a scorpion sting could kill you. I was so scared. I wondered if I should run to the station and tell my dad. I immediately pushed that idea out of my head. He'd beat me for leaving the shop.

So I leaned back on the shed, closed my eyes full of tears, expecting to die. My dad came back, and I didn't have the bolts out of the hitch, and he was overwhelmingly mad.

I told him what had happened and that I was going to die, crying my heart out. "You total dumbass!" he yelled. "The only thing that is going to kill you is *me*."

Then it started. He hit me in the face and knocked me down. *He really is going to kill me*, I thought. I figured either way—scorpion or Dad—death was imminent. I can't describe the fear of facing death and what it was doing to me.

After that beating, my heart was hardened even more. Not *completely* though. Close by, there lived a very poor family with fourteen kids, the Smith family.

Mr. Smith drove a tractor for several farmers. Mrs. Smith stayed home with kids. They had a son named Kenneth; he was a year older than me. I got in the habit of going to the Smith house and would walk to school with Kenneth.

At the northwest corner of the same block lived the Mathew family. They had *six* kids. Straight across the road, west, lived the Cunningham family. There were *thirteen* kids in that family. Evidently, there was something in the water in our town.

One Monday morning I went over to the Smith house to walk to school with Kenneth. I knocked on the door, and Kenneth came to the door, crying.

"What's wrong?" I asked.

"Look," he said, opening the door wider.

I looked inside and was surprised at what I saw. The house was in shambles. There was food everywhere and white flour on *everything*.

"What in the world happened?" I asked.

"This happened while we were at church last night," Kenneth said.

I watched as all thirteen of his siblings tried to clean with tears in their eyes. I was heartbroken to say the least. *How could anybody do this to this family?* I looked over to Mr. Smith. He looked like he was in shock.

"Mr. Smith, if I could do anything to help you, what would it be?" I asked.

"If I just had a cup of coffee, I could get my thoughts together," he replied.

Just then, one of Kenneth's little brothers brought Mr. Smith his best dress hat. Somebody had taken a crap in it. I simply could not believe it. I went from their house to the little corner grocery store. I had a dollar and twenty-five cents for lunch at school that week. I looked at a jar of instant coffee. It was ninety-five cents, plus tax.

1-800-4-A-CHILD
www.callingallhearts.com

I took the coffee to Mr. Smith, and he was so thankful that I would help him. I had money for lunch that day but didn't eat lunch the rest of the week. I felt so sorry for the family. I told no one what I had done, especially not my parents. I didn't want to get beaten for helping Mr. Smith.

The authorities were called in to investigate the destruction of their house. The sheriff's department sent two deputies to the school. We were all pulled into the office, three grades at a time, just the boys. Questions were asked about who might know something about the incident.

After a few minutes, one of the deputies walked over to Billy Bob Cunningham and asked him why he did it. He proclaimed that he did not do it. Then the deputy grabbed his leg and turned his foot toward his face and said, "This is flour caked up on the bottom of your shoe! Who helped you?"

Billy's brother Ricky was sitting next to him and spoke up. "I did."

The two were immediately expelled from school, and their parents were called in.

I couldn't understand why all of this violence was happening to me and around me. Why was God allowing this to go on? I just didn't understand it. I became even more irate, and my fuse became shorter and shorter.

There was a kid named Jerry Riley who would come to our house to play basketball with me. A friend and I had attached a goal to an electric pole nearby. I had always had a tremendous love for basketball. I was even pretty good!

Jerry and I started playing one-on-one basketball to practice. During a game, Jerry got frustrated because I was beating him badly. He decided to shove me. Big mistake on his part.

I drew my arm back and hit him in the face, hard, with my fist. He fell to the ground, blood gushing from his nose. He came at me again. I hit him for the second time. This time, though, he didn't get up. He lay on the ground while I watched him bleed. I felt no compassion for him at all. I left him there while I went to the corner grocery store to get a Coke.

The man running the store saw the fight from his store window. He said, "I want to be your manager, kid! We'd make a lot of money on the boxing circuit!"

We laughed as I finished my Coke. I went home feeling pretty tough, thinking nobody was ever going to beat me. I wouldn't tolerate it.

My dad came home that evening; he had heard about the fight. He asked me what happened, and I told him the truth. He then looked at me with squinted eyes and then hit me with the back of his hand.

"You stupid dumbass!" he screamed. "We do *not* fight in *this* house!"

At the moment, I couldn't believe what he had said. But looking back, I see he was right. There was never a *fight*. It was just him beating the hell out of us.

He then proceeded to pull an empty whiskey bottle out of a sack and broke it over my head. It cut me deep, on the right corner of my forehead. My mother came in and saw what happened. Back to the hospital we went.

Again, the entire drive there, my mother kept repeating, "If they ask you what happened, you tell them you fell on the porch."

I was getting sick of being told this. I was getting seriously depressed. I didn't think this madness would ever end.

At the hospital, they put twenty-two stitches in my head. I wondered why nobody at the hospital ever asked any questions.

When my mother and I got home that night, Dad met us at the door, and he hit my mother. She grabbed me and pushed me between her and him.

"Get him, Rodney!" she cried. My father grabbed me and literally threw me through the front door of the house. It cut my arm pretty good.

He told my mother, "Bandage him up! We can't take him to the hospital again."

She took me to the bathroom and bandaged my arm. It was bleeding very badly. Thirty-minutes later, she had to re-bandage it because of all the blood. She did this three more times before it stopped bleeding.

My thoughts, which had already been dark, were growing darker. All I could think of was killing my dad. How could I *ever* stop him any other way?

1-800-4-A-CHILD
www.callingallhearts.com

That night, I tried to keep my mind off those evil thoughts and went back to distracting myself with the language I had created.

"Vous, wov, vous…."

The Perfect Son

Was there something more
I could have done
To stop all the beatings
And be the perfect son?

I finally understand
It was never my fault.
I could do nothing to
Bring it to a halt.

No matter how hard I tried,
I just always felt tied
To the fact I was no good,
And always felt misunderstood.

I try always to do what's right,
But there are people who insist
That they push you into a fight,
Which becomes the fight for your life.

1-800-4-A-CHILD
www.callingallhearts.com

Chapter Eleven

One day, Dad decided we needed to fix a water leak under the house. He had me come with him out to a little building we had at the corner of the property. He started going through a bucket of pipe fittings. He told me to hand him a pipe wrench. I looked around for it, unsure of *exactly* what he needed. I guess he decided I wasn't moving fast enough. He reached for a piece of pipe about eighteen inches long and started screaming at me to move.

I tried to move out of the way. Dad was in a squatted position and took the long pipe he had grabbed and hit me in the shin. It hurt so badly. I thought for sure he had broken it. I fell to the ground, crying and screaming.

"Shut up," he said, walking over to me. He started kicking me while I was on the ground. I tried so hard not to cry, but my leg was hurting so badly I couldn't quit.

The entire time I was on the ground, he was screaming, "Get up, dumbass!"

I tried with everything inside me to get up, but my leg pain was hurting way too much. I later in life found out that he *had* broken my shinbone.

Since I didn't get up, he jerked me up from the ground and slammed me on the side of the shop building. "Walk," he said.

I tried, but I could barely put any weight on my right leg. I started walking with a very bad limp. Just then, my dog

1-800-4-A-CHILD
www.callingallhearts.com

T-Bone, who had heard me screaming, came running. My dad kicked him, sending the poor dog into the air.

A stranger drove by the property and started talking to my dad. T-Bone and I walked behind the shop and dragged ourselves to the back of the house. We crawled under the house and searched out a dry spot.

The house was up off the ground far enough that I could sit up when I got under there. I backed up against the wall. T-Bone crawled up in my lap. He started whimpering, and I started crying.

I put my arms around him and held him tightly. He was my only, true friend. That was one of several hundred trips we made under there, together, both in pain.

Several weeks later, my leg was *still* hurting. Whenever Dad caught sight of me limping, he'd beat me and kick me.

A while later, we were out behind the shop building. He was making me cut weeds with a hoe. Again, I wasn't moving fast enough for him.

He picked up a piece of heavy-duty extension cord and started whipping me with it across the back. I started screaming. I couldn't get away from him because my leg hurt so badly, I couldn't run.

"Shut up!" he screamed.

The pain was too great; I couldn't find the strength to stop crying. I fell to the ground, straining hard to avoid the pain. It didn't work. I felt like I was going to pass out. I started to get dizzy; things around me were spinning. I passed out, only to wake up to Dad pouring water on my face.

During this time, Dad was working at the granite company. He'd bring huge chunks of granite home in the back of his pickup, almost every day. He'd stack them in the back yard and let them pile up.

Then one day, he decided to move all these enormous pieces of rock to the *other* side of the yard. He told me to start moving them in my wagon after school. After school, I loaded my wagon with the smallest pieces first and took them to the other side of the yard and unloaded them.

Before school that morning, Dad warned me that I had better move ten wagonloads before he got home. You better believe I was hurrying as quickly as I could! I told myself that every load I hauled would have to be bigger than the first.

As I put them in my wagon, my arms started to shake under the weight. I couldn't believe how heavy these things were! I had already taken two loads and was working on the third, and I started straining. I heaved and breathed deep, mustering all the strength I could.

"Ugh!" I groaned as I dropped the piece in the wagon. Suddenly an intense pain shot up my right arm, all the way to my chest. I couldn't get my ring finger on my right hand out from under the rock. The pain was worse than any beating I had had up to that point in my life.

I squirmed and shimmied my finger until I finally got it free. When I looked down at my hand, I started screaming at the top of my lungs. My sisters came running.

"Rodney, what happened?" Shirley asked.

I couldn't speak. I just held up my hand. I watched as her face went white. Carolyn started to cry. "What should we do?" Shirley asked me.

"I don't know!" I cried. There was no way to reach our parents at work. Shirley had gone inside and brought me a couple of washcloths to try to stop the bleeding. My finger was split down both sides, and the nail was barely hanging on. I sat in a rocking chair on the front porch with my hand wrapped up in a rag. I could feel the blood pulsing and leaving my finger. I sat there, crying for nearly two hours, waiting for my parents to come home.

When my dad got home, he sauntered up the steps with a smirk on his face. He started laughing and called me stupid. My mother came up behind him and unwrapped my hand. She bit her lip.

"I'll be back," my dad said, turning to leave the porch.

"Wayne, we need to take him to the hospital," my mother said.

My dad just laughed. "That costs money," he said, and he walked away.

He returned a few minutes later with a can of liquid that smelled awful. "What is that?" I asked, looking at my mother.

"Kerosene," my dad replied. "It'll fix that stupid finger."

My dad had me soak my finger in the can for about two hours. After that, my mom came out and cleaned it up. I don't know how much pain a young person can handle before he blows a fuse and absolutely goes crazy, but I was near it.

1-800-4-A-CHILD
www.callingallhearts.com

The pain in my finger did not go away. I started struggling at school because I was in so much anguish. Maybe it wouldn't have been so bad had it been my toe or something. But this was my *finger*. I needed it to do everything—write, comb my hair, brush my teeth, and eat. Every one of these normal tasks was punctuated with deep, agonizing pain.

None of the teachers noticed my finger while I was at school. I was a little scared to tell anyone about it too. I knew if I did and a teacher called my parents, I'd get beaten for sure.

Five days after it happened, I begged my mother to please take me to the doctor. Finally, she convinced my dad that it was not getting better and I needed to see a doctor. This time, they both took me.

When we got to the clinic, the doctor asked, "Good Lord, when did this happen? How has it been treated?"

"It happened five days ago," my mother said. The doctor waited for his answer to the second question.

Finally, my dad said, "We soaked it in kerosene."

I couldn't believe what happened next. The doctor's face went red, and he started yelling at my father. "You had *no* business soaking that finger in kerosene! Why would you do that?"

"It had always been used as an old home remedy," my father replied, angry.

The doctor growled. "It's people like *you* who think they are smarter than doctors! I swear...and what's worse, you've caused considerable damage to this boy's finger!"

He kept letting my dad have it as he bandaged up my finger. "That old home remedy stopped when they changed the chemical structure of kerosene!"

The doctor had the nurse clean my finger and try to get rid of that horrendous smell. He covered the finger with merthiolate, a red-colored liquid that turned my finger orange. He told me it was an antiseptic and antifungal agent. He then wrapped my finger where the bandage could be taken off every day.

He told my mother to get some Epson salt and mix it with water to try and get the finger clean. That should help it start to heal.

So every day that bandage came off and that finger got soaked in Epsom salt. This went on for an entire year before it ever got to where I could use that finger again.

To this day I can't stand the smell of Epsom salt. My finger is *still* messed up because of the kerosene.

My biggest disappointment out of the whole ordeal was not being able to play basketball at school. Basketball was practically the only thing I could enjoy in life, and I couldn't even do that.

I was stupid enough to think maybe because of my finger and the tongue-lashing the doctor gave my dad that beatings would stop. Boy, was I ever mistaken! I still had to work with a messed up finger and all. The beatings just kept on going and going and going.

One of the most severe after the finger incident was when we were in the shop in the backyard. Again, I wasn't moving fast enough for my dad. He picked up a strand of bailing wire and locked the door to the shop. The building was twenty feet by twenty feet with nowhere to run.

He started whipping me with that steel wire as hard as he could. The pain was unbelievable. It made me think about the story of Jesus, getting whipped with the cat-o'-nine-tails, right before the crucifixion[1].

I fell to the ground and curled up in a ball. He kept beating me with the bailing wire, showing no mercy whatsoever. He started screaming, "Stop that crying!" This time, I did. Only because I blacked out and could no longer feel any pain.

My Best Was Never Good Enough

I did my best.
It was never good enough.
He accused me of
Always messing up.

I spent years trying to
figure out why it was me,
just assuming that's the
way it had to be.

I wanted to quit.

1 John 19:1

1-800-4-A-CHILD
www.callingallhearts.com

I wanted to walk away.
I heard a voice one day
That said you have to stay.

～

So stay I did.
That voice again saying,
"You did nothing wrong."
When I realized this,
I started to become strong.

1-800-4-A-CHILD
www.callingallhearts.com

Chapter Twelve

When I was about twelve years old, my dad's brother and his family moved to Hollister. They moved into a brick building complex, right off the highway. The south end of the building was two stories. They put a grocery store in the downstairs area and lived above it.

I'd stop in sometimes to visit or just hide from my dad. I was in the back of the store one day, and my stomach was growling. I was so hungry. Food at our house was not plentiful. I saw some bananas nearby and decided to eat one. I had never had a banana, and I really wanted to try one.

I peeled one halfway and started eating. My cousin Jack heard me, came around the corner, and caught me. I was so hungry that his presence didn't stop me. I knew I'd be in trouble, but at the time, all I could think about was getting *something* in my stomach.

Jack took me to the front of the store to his older brother, Chester, and told him what I had done. I immediately started begging them not to tell their dad or my dad. I had tears in my eyes, scared beyond belief. I kept begging and begging, but I couldn't tell if they were listening to me or not.

I went home as scared as I had ever been. When I actually did something that was wrong, waiting was so much worse. I was scared all night and the entire next day. When my dad got home, he sent me out to pick up trash behind the shop building.

I was picking up trash when I saw him coming around the corner and looked at his hands. My heart sank. He had picked up two strands of bailing wire and was walking toward me with a menacing look in his eye.

"Why'd you steal that banana?"

"I was starving, Daddy," I said, tensing up. "I couldn't resist."

Then, it happened. He started whaling on me with the steel bailing wire. I'm not sure I could describe the pain that came with it. I had cried all I could. There were no tears left. I tensed up as hard as I could, trying to absorb the horrific pain.

He finally quit when he saw blood coming through the back of my shirt. "Get in the house, you little bastard."

I ran inside and locked myself in the bathroom. The next day, I went back to the store and asked Jack why he told on me. He said, "It wasn't me. It was Chester."

I didn't say anything. I turned around and lifted up my shirt. I heard Jack gasp.

"What happened to you?" Jack asked.

"This is what my dad did to me because Chester told on me," I said, pulling my shirt down and turning back around.

"Wayne did that to you?" he asked.

I nodded. "He took some bailing wire and doubled it and started beating me. He asked why I took the banana, and I told him I was so hungry I couldn't keep from eating it."

We were both quiet for a moment.

"Jack, I'm sorry," I said. "I wouldn't have eaten it, but I hadn't eaten since the day before."

He looked at me and said, "I never thought anything like this would happen."

He took me to the back of the store where the bananas were stored and snapped four off of a bunch. Then he led me out the back door, and we went to an old grain bin and ate two bananas each. My God, they were absolutely the most delicious things I had ever eaten.

When I started home, I was feeling a little bit better. I had some food in my stomach—bananas no less—and felt I had someone on my side. That's when I felt a small rock hit me in the back of the head. I spun around and saw Bobby Dismukes.

Bobby was two years older than me and a thorn in my side. I looked more like his family than I did any of the Timms; both of us were red headed and had freckles. I was constantly being called a Dismukes, which I totally resented.

"Why'd you throw a rock at me?" I said, anger boiling up.

"Because I damn well wanted to," Bobby said, smirking.

"Don't let it happen again!" I yelled at him and was about to turn to go when he started toward me.

"Shut your damn mouth!" he said.

As soon as he came close enough, I hit him right smack in the mouth. He hit the ground hard. "You'd better stay down," I said. Bobby got back up, and I knocked him back down. That's when I saw his older brother coming at me. His name was David, and he was the same age as my cousin Jack.

1-800-4-A-CHILD
www.callingallhearts.com

I started to panic because he was a lot bigger than me. I looked over my shoulder and saw my cousin Jack. He met David in the street, head on, and hit him in the face, knocking him down. The fight was on!

Bobby came at me again. I knocked him to the ground for the third time. This time I pinned his shoulders to the ground and started beating him in the face. My hands were completely covered in blood.

All of a sudden, someone pulled me off him. It was my uncle, Junior. My grandpa was C.H. Timms Sr., and my uncle was named C.H. Timms Jr. But everyone called him "Junior."

Junior pulled me off Bobby and pushed me to the ground. "Leave him alone!" Then, he went over and hit Jack in the back of the head with his fist. Jack fell backward on the ground. Bobby and David took off running home. I'm glad Jack was there to keep both of them from beating me up really bad.

About three weeks later, I was having problems with a kid three years older than me by the name of Tommy Cunningham. He was the oldest brother of the two boys who destroyed the Smith house. Tommy always came across as a tough guy. I couldn't stand him. What made matters worse was he was a cousin of *my cousin*, Jack.

I knew there would never be any backup from Jack; their mothers were sisters. I was afraid of Tommy because he kept pushing me around. He had it in for me; my dad had beaten his dad up three or four times.

1-800-4-A-CHILD
www.callingallhearts.com

Sunday night, me and a bunch of other kids were at the First Baptist Church of Hollister. My mom and dad rarely went to church, but my sisters and I always did because that was a place we felt safe. This particular night, Tommy Cunningham was at church, sitting in the row behind me.

Some kids were asking for songbooks, and I was passing them back to them. Tommy was walking in the aisle and said I hit him between the legs. I told him he was crazy; I never touched him, and he knew that. He then told me to meet him outside after church; he was going to kick my ass.

I didn't say a word because I was scared out of my mind. It seemed like church was over in five minutes, when it really lasted two hours. I hurried outside and hooked up with my sisters who had their boyfriends with them. I thought when he saw all of them he would leave me alone. Wrong.

I could hear him walking up behind me with four of his buddies. He came up in front of me and said, "Do you want to fight in the road or move over in the grass where it is softer?"

The road consisted of red clay with big old rocks in it. Before Tommy could say another word, I hit him with my left hand and knocked him to the ground on the rough, old road. I promise you from the look in his eyes if he hadn't had his buddies, he would never have gotten up. But he did, and the fight was on. I kept hitting him harder and harder. He tried to hit me but couldn't. I had his arm twisted behind him and was hitting him in the face.

I backed him half a city block, all the way to the edge of the church property. I pushed him into the drainage ditch

1-800-4-A-CHILD
www.callingallhearts.com

and went after him. That's when he kicked me in the mouth. I touched my lip and saw blood on my fingertips. That was the only blood he drew from me.

I grabbed him and took him to the ground, pinning him with my knees, and started beating his face. All of a sudden, someone started pulling on me. I was not going to let go. Then I felt someone grab me from the other side, dragging me off Tommy. He was taken to the hospital where he was treated for a broken right hand. He had forty-two stitches to his face and head.

By this time, my sisters started yelling and screaming at me.

"Rodney!" Carolyn screamed, throwing her hands in the air. "Why do you keep doing this?"

"Yeah!" Shirley said. "We can't have any friends because you beat everybody up!"

They kept screaming at me the whole two-block walk home. I started crying, thinking my sisters hated me, and it wasn't even my fault. I went in to the house to the bathroom to wash my face. I heard my mother yelling at me at the top of her lungs.

"You little bastard! All you want to do is fight!"

She followed me into the bathroom, screaming the whole time. I washed my face and wiped it with a towel, trying to control my anger. Finally, I had had enough.

I turned to her with my fist doubled up. "I've had enough!" I said. "You should just leave me alone."

"You better not touch me," she said, her eyes narrowing.

"You'd better back up," I said, moving closer to her. "I've had way too much. I can't take any more!"

She looked into my eyes and then down to my fists. "Wayne!" she hollered over her shoulder. "Wayne! This bastard son of yours is gonna hit me!"

My dad walked in, and my mother started running her mouth. "He would have hit me if I wouldn't have called for you!" she said.

"Look at me, boy!" my dad said.

When I did, he hit me square in the jaw. I fell over into the old cast iron bathtub. It hurt so badly; for a moment I thought my back had been broken. He jerked me up by my arm and slammed me into the door. I fell backward, covered in blood, and started crying my heart out.

The entire time he was kicking or hitting me, yelling, "You'd better quit fighting!" All the while I was thinking, *My parents are so stupid! Don't they know I'm like this because of* him? It's a miracle I never became a sociopathic killer, and believe me, I came very close.

After that night, Tommy Cunningham and his brothers never bothered me again. Of course, my whole family hated me now. My sisters were mad because I fought people they wanted to be friends with. My mom hated me because I fought too much. And my dad hated me because…well, I still didn't know the answer to that. I guess because he just wanted to.

That night, I decided I was going to have to kill my dad. I couldn't take fighting a kid and then *him* beating me. I decided I had no choice.

The next morning, as usual, Roy Grant called my dad and asked him if I could help him in his fields. Thankfully, my dad said yes. I got to help him for three straight weeks. I started thinking I just might make it.

While I worked in the fields, I wished I could be Roy Grant's son. He was such a nice man. He had such patience teaching the skills of farming. What an angel.

The Walking Dead

I was no match
for his gigantic size.
I walked around
With two black eyes.

In the summer I walked
Around in a long-sleeved shirt.
If I told anybody,
He would knock me to the dirt.

To beat me all the time
Seemed to be his style.
He even beat me if
I just tried to smile.

1-800-4-A-CHILD
www.callingallhearts.com

I had bright hair
That was extremely red.
He humiliated me so much
I considered myself
The walking dead.

1-800-4-A-CHILD
www.callingallhearts.com

Chapter Thirteen

Hollister had done away with their high school. So when I got through the eighth grade, we had to go to another town to go to school. I'm proud to say I was valedictorian of my eighth grade class. Granted, there were only four of us, but still. I only made it because they didn't count our conduct grades.

Because Hollister had no high school, students had the choice of going to school in Frederick or Chattanooga. I really wanted to go to Frederick to play football to take out my aggression. I was fast and very strong. When I told my parents what I wanted to do, they said, "You're not going to school with blacks."

Around this time, my dad opened up a shop and salvage in Chattanooga. That soon became my home away from home. I had to constantly work there night and day. Dad would keep me there many nights until three or four in the morning. He'd go to the bar by eight or nine in the evening. He would leave me at the shop to work with no food and no water.

I would get extremely hungry and have no money and no way to get food. I was given work to do each time he left. I'd have to stay hooked up to get it all done. One night, I thought I would set down to relax for a few minutes, and I fell into a deep sleep. The next thing I knew, my dad was waking me up.

He had a beer in his hand and poured it on me. I was so mad. "What did you do that for?" I screamed.

He backhanded me and knocked me to the floor. I started to get up, and then he kicked me. I rolled up in a ball as he kicked me again.

"Get your ass up and get in the pickup," he growled.

As I climbed in, he got behind the wheel. He was so drunk he could barely function. It scared me badly. We pulled out on the main highway, and a Dodge Charger pulled up beside us. We were in an old '55 Chevy pickup that my dad had just put a brand new 327 engine in. The Charger revved its engine, and my dad responded. I could see we were going to race.

As we pulled up, the Dodge took off, and we stayed right with him. I was shaking, terrified because my dad was so drunk. We pulled past the Charger and beat him. Personally, I think the Charger let us win because he too was afraid of what my dad would do to him if he lost. He waved off the Dodge, and we went on down the highway. We turned and pulled into Uncle Junior's drive. My dad parked and went to the porch. He started banging loudly on the door. My uncle came to the door, and my dad started yelling at him.

"You're an asshole! Not doin' business with my garage!"

After some yelling back and forth, my dad came back to the pickup and got in. "My brother is a no-good son of a bitch. He's just like everybody else in the world. They want your help but don't want to help you!" He started preaching to me about the world that could go to hell for all he cared. There wasn't one good person left on the planet.

I was sitting on my side of the vehicle, tense and scared. I just knew he was going to start beating on me. As soon as the

1-800-4-A-CHILD
www.callingallhearts.com

thought entered my mind, it happened. He started slapping me in the chest and stomach, telling me I was a no-good son of a bitch like the rest of the world.

I kept trying to think of someone I could run off to and not have to worry about it anymore. But there was no one. This was too much extreme stress for any young person. My stomach was always upset and hurting. I found it hard to swallow when he was around. I never had the opportunity to relax and get my mind off what he was doing to me.

After school let out that summer, I had to go back to the shop in Chattanooga. The city was building a new road through Chattanooga. My dad struck up a deal with the owner of the trucks working on the road to fix the truck's flats.

I had to break the tires down off the wheel. I had a ten-pound sledgehammer with the handle cut off so I could swing it like a hammer. I swung this hammer all day long. We averaged fixing thirty flats a day. I was an extremely strong kid. After that summer, I had gotten a whole lot stronger.

One day it rained, and we didn't have to fix any truck flats. We had an old Minneapolis Moline tractor in the shop. My dad had taken two tractors and made one tractor. We were putting on the back tires and wheels. My dad gave me a lug wrench and a round tire tool for a handle. He told me to tighten the nuts on the lugs.

I twisted one off, which shocked me. My dad started screaming and yelling at me and knocked me to the floor. I got back up as quickly as I could.

"You ought to be more careful!"

1-800-4-A-CHILD
www.callingallhearts.com

I'm only twelve years old, I thought. *I should not be able to twist off a five-eighth-inch bolt.*

I gathered myself together and got back to tightening the bolts up. As hard as I tried, I couldn't keep myself from twisting another one off. My dad heard it happen and came running. He started hitting me and kicking me. I couldn't take anymore. I took off running.

I got to the workbench and stopped. I picked up a two-and-a-half-foot brake over and stuck it in his face. "If you don't leave me alone, I'll kill you!"

"Put it down!" he yelled.

"No!" I said. "I mean it! I'll kill you!"

He stared me down, and I stared back. I lost my nerve and dropped the brake over and took off running out the door. As I ran down the street, I heard my dad get in his pickup and come after me. He rolled the window down and called after me.

"Come on, Rodney," he said. "Get back in the car. Let's not fight."

I couldn't believe he was trying to make amends with me. I was so starved for love that I gave in and got in the pickup. By the time we got back to the shop, he had already started preaching to me that I would never amount to a hill of beans. That didn't matter too much to me; I had learned to tune him out. At least he wasn't beating me. I had other people to take care of that.

Jesse Blair was one of those people. He always ran around acting like he could whip the world. He would push me to the point of fighting and then would disappear. Jesse Blair was actually the kid who shot Terry Bradley when we were younger. His dad, Frank, was one of the men who stabbed Hunk Rich. Of course, Frank didn't have to go to jail because his brother-in-law was the sheriff. Jesse never got in trouble, even though he was just as bad as his dad. The apple sure didn't fall far from *that* tree.

Jesse ran around beating up on little kids. He never seemed to fight anybody his own age. He was two years older than me. And at the ripe old age of fourteen, Jesse drank a lot of beer and thought it made him Superman. Back then, beer could be bought in the town of Frederick at any age. Times were rough, and everybody was about making money, so the age limit was hardly ever enforced.

One particular night, Jesse and four of his buddies were following me home from working at my dad's shop. They had been egging on Tommy Cunningham, trying to get him riled up before they set their sights on me. Jesse was heckling me, big time.

"Knock it off, Jesse," I said. "I don't have any intention of fighting all five of you."

He kept on, poking me and saying things like, "Come on, what's the matter? You scared?"

"Shut up and leave me alone," I said.

"Come on, chicken shit," Jesse said.

I wasn't afraid of Jesse and his friends because of the beatings I had been through. I didn't think all five of them could hurt me as badly as I had been hurt before. I turned, squared

1-800-4-A-CHILD
www.callingallhearts.com

up with him, and hit him in the face with my right hand. He hit the ground hard.

Jesse jumped back up, and I knocked him down again. It was at that moment that one of his buddies tripped me. I hit the ground with a thud. I didn't have time to brace myself for the fall. Jesse jumped on me, and so did one of his buddies. The third guy started kicking.

Guys who think they are tough never know what to do with a person who has been beaten all their life. I started kicking the three of them as they tried to hurt me. I swung both arms and started kicking both feet. I knew I had the upper hand.

About that time my dad walked out on the porch of our house. "Let's get out of here!" Jesse called, springing to his feet and gesturing to his friends.

"You don't need to leave," said my dad. "I'm just going to watch."

"Oh no," Jesse said, shaking his head. "I've heard about you! You're mean. I don't want to have anything to do with you."

"Come back," my dad said. "Carry on as you were."

As Jesse and his friends ran off, I started in the house. "Get your ass in the house and get cleaned up," said my dad as I walked past him. My mother met me in the kitchen.

"You no-good bastard. Don't you see you're just like him?" she said, slapping me across the face.

My lip was already bleeding, and with the slap, blood went everywhere. She started screaming at me. I was ready to hit her. I couldn't take it anymore. About that time, my dad rounded the corner into the kitchen and hit me in the back of the head. I fell to the floor. He started screaming at me to leave my mother alone. I told him to tell her to leave me alone. He kicked me in the head and knocked me out. I woke up the next morning lying in the kitchen floor.

After that night, Jesse Blair never bothered me again. About three years later, we wound up working together for D.C. Wilson, cutting and bailing hay. We never had a problem. Then, a couple of years later, Jesse moved to Colorado and came back with a bad attitude and three buddies to back him up. They wreaked havoc on *everyone*. None of them ever fought alone, it was always the four of them.

One night in Frederick, at the Sonic Drive-In, they beat up a friend of mine, Terry Hendricks. They beat him senseless. I heard about it the next morning and went to talk to Terry's older brother, Jimmy.

"Jimmy, can you get your hands on a twelve-gauge shotgun?" I asked.

"Sure," he said. "Are we going to kill them?"

"That's up to them!" I replied.

We knew that Jesse and his buddies always hung out at Sonic. They didn't have anything better to do than sit around the drive in, waiting to hurt someone. I had Jimmy meet me across the street at 8:30 p.m. that night. He was right on time.

"All right," I said. "Here's how this needs to go down. I'm going over there to get Jesse out of the car. You hold the shotgun on his three buddies. If they act like they are going to

1-800-4-A-CHILD
www.callingallhearts.com

move, fire the gun in the air and tell them if it goes off again it will be at one of their heads!"

Jimmy nodded in agreement.

We went across the street, and I saw Jesse sitting behind the wheel. At that time, he had a full beard. I walked over to his open window and reached through and grabbed him by the beard.

Jimmy stuck the shotgun in the back window. "Anybody moves, they're dead," he said.

I pulled Jesse through the driver's door window by the beard. As he hit the ground, I had two hands full of beard. I jumped on him, pinned his shoulders to the concrete, and started beating him out of his mind. About that time, I heard the shotgun go off.

Then I heard Jimmy say, "The next one will take somebody's head off!"

I beat Jesse unconscious, got up, and told one of the carhops to call an ambulance. To this day, I have not heard a word from Jesse Blair. It was at that moment that I became afraid of myself.

Where Were the Good Ole Days

What happened to
The good ole days,
When kids were
Allowed to play?

1-800-4-A-CHILD
www.callingallhearts.com

I can't remember
Them at all.
I just remember
Every time I would fall.

I spent most of my time
Just trying to hide,
Knowing this could be
The day that I died.

I wanted to run;
I wanted to have fun;
I was destined for fear,
While he drank his beer.

Chapter Fourteen

There was a prominent family that lived near the town of Hollister named Kinder. They raised Hereford cattle. One of the men in the family was Donald "Red Eye" Kinder. He drove a car around that was always overloaded with clothes. He played in a country band and traveled all over the country. One day, a new kid showed up at school by the name of Valton Gambil. He was the son of "Red-Eye" Kinder.

I didn't like him.

Because I didn't like him, I started to bully him. It was my nature; I didn't like it, but I had no control over it. Yes, that's what I said: absolutely no control. My rage had started coming out because of what was happening to me at home. The torture and the beatings were destroying me. I was well on my way to becoming a sociopath. That's a person who has been traumatized, and because of that, they start feeling no remorse for hurting people.

I decided I wanted to run Valton Gambil out of our school. To be honest, I hate to admit it; I really wanted to kill him. I did *not* want him around. So every day at school, I would walk up to him and shove him. He would just look at me and turn and walk away. This made me even madder.

I would go after him, curse at him, and push him again. I kept thinking if he would just fight me I could beat him to death. I *needed* to hurt somebody. I spent the next two years trying to get Valton to fight me, and he wouldn't. I called him names, insulted him, pushed him, shoved him, and bullied him. But he absolutely would not fight me.

Then he started hanging out with a local girl in Hollister named Shirley Mathews. That really made me mad. He was an outsider! Why should he get the cutest, sweetest girl in town? I had my eye on her already! But it wasn't meant to be. Valton was a good guy. I was the bad guy. It was my nature to be that way; I couldn't help myself.

Valton Gambil and Shirley Mathews eventually got married. Valton went to college and became an accountant. They moved to south-central Oklahoma near the town of Waurika. There they raised a son, Curtis. He was in and out of a lot of juvenile detention centers in his youth. When Curtis was a high school student, he became overwhelmingly mean. He was always out shooting people's dogs in their own front yards. He also spent time driving around out in the country shooting cows and horses. He seemed to *enjoy* it. He was never convicted of any crime, though. Apparently, he was a psychopath—born without a conscious in other words. He felt absolutely no remorse.

He teamed up with two Waurika High School boys and drugged a sixteen-year-old cheerleader. They took her south of Waurika into Texas, down into a creek where Curtis and his grandmother used to fish, and raped her. They stopped on a bridge to make her get out and walk, but Curtis took out a twelve-gauge shotgun, shot her nine times, and pushed her down in the river. It was devastating to the people of that part of the state.

They were all tried in Texas and incarcerated in Texas. Just a few years later, they broke out of prison. For ten days after, Valton and Shirley's home was infiltrated with US Marshals.

It was then that I really felt bad for Valton and Shirley. They were both really good people and certainly didn't deserve that. I'm sure they felt bad for the family of the young cheer-leader, too.

I really started feeling bad for Valton Gambil. I know he was a good guy because he never would fight me. I never have apologized to him. Maybe one day I can apologize, let him know that it was never his fault.

I was on my way home from school one day, by myself. My sisters didn't want me walking with them. I cut through the Rackley family's backyard. I had been through their backyard several times, and I kept noticing this orange boxcar from an electric train laying in the dirt. I was mesmerized by it. I had never seen anything like it. I wanted it so badly. One day, I decided I would take it. After all, I saw my dad take things time after time after time.

When I cut through their backyard, I grabbed it, shoved it in my pocket, and went on my way. When I got it home, I put it in my room. Later, my sister saw it and asked me about it. I told her the wind blew it in the yard.

"Liar," she said.

I knew I was in trouble. I immediately started praying she wouldn't tell my dad. I looked at the boxcar and was so caught up in how neat it was, I traveled away from the fear inside of me. I thought if I had the whole train how cool it would be.

The fear bounced right back inside of me when I heard the back door shut. I kept thinking, *Please don't tell him. Please don't tell him.* Naturally, she told him. I think she must have thought it would keep him away from her.

Dad sat down on the couch with a bottle of whiskey and started drinking. Fear ripped my insides apart. I sat quietly on my bed, hoping and praying he would not come in my room. About that time, I heard Mother holler, "Suppertime!"

Here we go, I thought.

I walked straight by my dad and on to my place at the kitchen table. We ate while my dad drank his supper straight from the bottle. When we finished eating, which didn't take long, as my stomach was twisted in knots, my dad took his bottle of whiskey to the couch and hollered at me.

I'm dead.

He told me to get a small bowl from the kitchen. I took it to him. Then he told my mother to cut up a pork chop from supper and bring it to him. He put it in the bowl then filled the bowl with whiskey.

"T-Bone!" he called. "T-Bone!" He whistled, waiting for the dog. T-Bone came in and hopped over to my dad. My dad stuck the bowl under his nose. To my surprise T-Bone started drinking the whiskey and eating the pork chop! I sat there on the couch watching T-Bone stagger off. I was worried about him; he was my best friend.

What if he turns mean, too?

"Now," my dad said, turning to me, "bring me this thing that 'blew into the yard.'"

I went to my room and grabbed the train car. I took it to Dad, and he immediately grabbed it out of my hands. "Bullshit!" he said. "This thing didn't blow anywhere." He reached out and hit me, knocking me clear across the room.

"You're a damn liar!" he yelled.

"No, I'm not, Daddy!" I said.

He knocked me backward. I fell on the boxcar and heard it bust into many pieces. One piece gouged my back, and it started to bleed. My dad walked over to me and beat me over and over. I started crying; that made him beat me more.

I could not stop crying. He looked at me as I lay out on the floor and said, "You are a total idiot. I'll give you one more chance to tell me the truth, and I'll quit hitting you."

"It came out of the yard across the street," I said in between sobs.

"Oh yeah?" he snarled. "Pick up those pieces and pile it up in the yard it came from!"

I started to sit up so I could gather up the broken remnants of the train. I gathered them up and piled them in a nearby yard. When I walked back into the house, he started yelling at me again.

"You're a no-good, piece-of-shit thief!"

Hypocrite, I thought as I passed him.

Just as I cleared the door inside, he hit me again. He told me he wouldn't, but he did. I should have known he wouldn't keep his word. He started hitting and kicking me. My back was already bleeding, as were my lips.

Finally, he left me alone to go back to his bottle. I sat on the floor, shaking uncontrollably. My mother ran me some bath water and told me to go use it. I sat down in the water and started crying, unable to stop.

Nobody seems to care if I live or die! I thought. *So why not just die? Surely heaven's got to be better than this?*

As I cried in the tub, my thoughts turned dark and bleak. Finally, I decided it was either him or me. I made a plan that night to get the gun from the closet. I told myself I'd decide who died later that night.

I finally got out of the tub and made my way to my bedroom, struggling with the decision as to whether I should kill him or myself. My mind was running wild.

I need to lie down first, I told myself. *Then I can think.* I lay down. It felt like my head had just hit the pillow when my mother shook me. It was already the next morning.

"You can't go to school today," she said as I jolted awake. "You don't even think about going outside, you hear me?"

She left my room, and I overheard her talking to my sisters. "You tell everyone he's sick, you hear me? Tell them he has a fever."

I didn't go to school for seven days. It took that long for my bruises to go away and wounds to heal.

No One Ever Took My Side

I just wanna cry
Because no one ever
Takes me side.
I wish they could
Just feel my pain.

It's somehow like
An irremovable stain.
It wasn't my fault
I was beat by my father
And not protected by my mother.

I just want to die inside
'Cause no one understands why I cry.
No one cares about my hurt.
They just want to treat me
Like I'm dirt.

When I feel like I can't go on
And my heart begins to turn to stone,
I'm reminded that I'm loved
When He reaches down from above.
He is my Savior
And helps me control my behavior.

1-800-4-A-CHILD
www.callingallhearts.com

Chapter Fifteen

Later that year, we traveled to Ada where my mother's mother lived. We called her "Granny Stiles"; she was so sweet to me. I loved her so much; she was so good to me. The trips to see her were so nice. I didn't have to worry about my dad beating me with a crowd.

We started the trip in an old '57 Chevy. By the time we got to Lawton, it was running badly. My dad said he needed some tools, so we pulled into a place called Surplus City. It started out as an army surplus, but as the years went by, they added tools, fishing gear, and garden supplies.

My dad went in to get some wrenches so he could work on the car. As he left the store and opened the car door, a man hollered at him and said, "What about those wrenches you put in your pocket?"

"What about them?" my dad yelled back.

"I think you better come back into the store before we call the police!" said the man.

Dad turned and went back inside. Nothing was said amongst my sisters, my mother, and me. In about fifteen minutes, he came back and got in the car. He didn't say a single word. We went to another parts store, and he bought some wrenches, eventually getting the car fixed.

We drove on to Ada and got there about eleven o'clock at night. We went straight to bed when we arrived. The next

1-800-4-A-CHILD
www.callingallhearts.com

morning, everybody but Granny Stiles and I went to town. We were sitting in the living room, just the two of us.

"Granny?"

"Yes, sweetie?"

"Something happened last night," I said, squirming in my seat.

"What happened, dear?" she asked.

I told her everything that happened: the car breaking down, Daddy going into the store, stealing the wrenches, and getting caught.

"Are you sure that's what happened, Rodney?" she asked, a little taken aback.

"Yes, ma'am, Granny," I assured her. "That's what happened."

She questioned me over and over, having me repeat the story again and again. My dad had always made her think he was the perfect son-in-law, and she thought he was until I told her about the stealing. I wanted so badly to tell her about the beatings, but I couldn't. It was hard enough trying to convince her that my dad was a thief.

When the rest of the family got home, Granny asked my mother if the story was true. I watched my mother's face get red and saw her start to breathe heavily. "No, Mother," said my mom, "it's *not* true."

Oh my God, I thought. *I'm going to die.* Right then I *knew* I couldn't tell Granny Stiles about the beatings. I would wind up dead. *You might wind up that way anyhow*, I thought.

The next day, we started home right after lunch. As we loaded up in the car, my dad told my mother to ride in the back with my sisters. Fear gripped my heart. *Here it comes*, I thought. *He's going to kill me and shove me out of a moving car.*

After we got in the car, waved bye to Granny Stiles, and drove a few blocks, my dad hit me across the face with the back of his hand. My nose started bleeding profusely. Dad stopped the car and screamed at my mother to get out and help me.

"Can I have your handkerchief, Wayne?" she asked.

"No!" he yelled. "I don't want *his* blood all over it. Get a rag from the trunk!"

My mom walked around to the back of the car and came back with a greasy rag. She held it on my nose until it stopped bleeding. That rag stunk badly.

"Get in back, dumbass!" my dad yelled to me. "Vida, get in the front!"

I got in the back and sat by my sisters. As we drove off, my dad started lecturing me about minding my own business, saying, "Next time, you might die."

I withdrew inside myself, seriously depressed and wondering if it would ever stop. I just sat there like a zombie, not knowing where to go or what to do. I kept telling myself that I didn't have the heart to kill, but that was rapidly changing.

That fall, I started the ninth grade in Chattanooga. Being a freshman felt like a big deal. The only thing I didn't like about going to school there was that my dad had his shop and salvage in the same town. That meant that's where I would have to go every day after school. I hated being around my dad. The truth is, I totally hated him.

Meanwhile, back at Hollister I had some buddies I hung out with. I'd slip out the window of my bedroom, and we'd meet at an old, abandoned house on the south side of town. We would sit out on the old front porch and talk. One of my buddies talked about going into Frederick on Saturdays and stealing things from stores. We all decided that the next Saturday we would all try it.

I already got to go to town with my mother on Saturdays to help with groceries and anything else she needed, so I'd at least have a ride. When Saturday rolled around, I asked my mom if I could go with her into town and go to the pool hall and shoot pool. She said yes but told me to be back in an hour.

I met my buddies at White's Automotive. We made our plan and walked inside. As soon as I saw the coast was clear, I started putting tools of all kinds into my pockets. I headed out the door where my friends were already waiting on me.

We went into the alley and started comparing the loot. I, by far, had the most. Wasn't hard, I was taught by the best. We put all the stuff in one my friend's brother's car. That was the only way we could get it back home without anyone seeing anything. We did this for the next three weeks.

On the fourth Saturday, I was sick and couldn't go. I found out that the others got busted. They were actually in serious trouble. The shop owner said he knew there was usually a fourth boy with them and asked who the other accomplice was. None of them ever told anybody that it was me. They wound up with six months probation. I decided after that I wouldn't steal anymore. I didn't want to get caught.

As I started my first weeks at Chatty High School, I was very standoffish. I never talked much to people I didn't know. One day, I was walking down the crowded hall at school when all of a sudden I got pushed to the floor by one of the seniors. I gave him a "go to hell look" and walked off.

The next week we were in the gym for junior high basketball. In came another senior, and he decided he was going to play with us. He was such a jerk, acting like he owned the place just because he was older. I was really getting sick of these seniors acting like they were gods.

"Get your ass out of here," I told him when he took the basketball from a friend. "You're not supposed to be here."

"Is that so?" he asked, and he threw the basketball behind him. He walked over to the side of the court and grabbed a mop, left there by the janitor. He ran up to me and hit me with it. I immediately grabbed him and threw him up against the railing of the bleachers. He bounced off with a thud and fell to the floor.

I walked over to him and stood above him. "You done?" I asked. He quickly scrambled to his feet and ran out. I was feeling pretty good about myself. I even walked to my dad's shop after school with a smile on my face.

When I walked in, my dad came up behind me with a 2-x-4 piece of wood and hit me right in the middle of the back. I went to my knees and then hit the floor. I started crying as usual.

"Shut up or I'll give you some more!" he said. I lay there for a little while, all tensed up; then he made me get up. I thought my back was broken.

1-800-4-A-CHILD
www.callingallhearts.com

"I heard about your fight," he said. "That kid you walloped, his dad and I drink together. I won't have you ruining my life! Every time you get in a fight you're gonna get some of this!" He held the board in his hand. Needless to say, I didn't smile the rest of the day.

The very next day I was sitting in a booth at Chappell's Café with some friends, eating lunch. A short, stocky kid named Tom hit me in the back of the head. I jumped out of the booth and put my cigarette out in his left eye. He kicked me in the stomach and knocked the wind out of me. He beat on me while I tried to catch my breath, lying in the floor gasping for air. He walked out the door when I finally caught my breath and got up. *I'm going to kill him*, I thought as I watched him walk down the street.

Two weeks later, we were in the baseball dugout at school, and he pushed me. I grabbed a thirty-three-inch Ernie Banks baseball bat in one hand and his throat in the other. I shoved the bat under his nose and told him, "You touch me again, and I will kill you."

I guess I convinced him; he never ever bothered me again. He later became a police officer in Chattanooga and stopped me several times for speeding but never wrote me a ticket.

Think Good Thoughts

To get depressed
Just think bad thoughts,

Or maybe about all those
Battles you've fought.

But refuse
To always think bad.
Think of all the good times
That you have had.

Learn to laugh
And have fun.
Don't think about
Having to run.

Dwell on everything
That is good.
Do what is right,
Do what you should.

Always be happy,
Refuse to lose.
Trust me,
Life will then go smoothly.

1-800-4-A-CHILD
www.callingallhearts.com

Chapter Sixteen

I started getting more and more depressed. I just couldn't do anything right. I started begging God to relieve the pain; it had just overwhelmed me. All I could think about was, *Why me? Am I that bad of a person?*

My thoughts soon started turning to anger. Beating after beating, the rage started growing deeper inside of me. It had started coming out of my mouth. I started to *try* to make people mad so they would fight me. That brought on more beatings at the hands of my father. I started begging God to kill him.

I would sit on the side of my bed, crying and begging God, *Please kill him! Please, God, the pain is too much. I can't take it anymore!* My anger became uncontrollable. I quit waiting on people to fight me. I started fights by just walking up and hitting a person in the face as hard as I could and watching them fall. Most people never got back up. Those that did got the whipping of their lives.

I was extremely strong for my age. Fighting and swinging a ten-pound sledgehammer for two summers and breaking down truck tires will help a boy gain some muscle. My tough-guy reputation got around pretty quickly. I was fighting three to five times a week and wasn't losing.

Somehow that made me feel much better. I was taking my aggression out on someone else. I became very intimidating to people. I learned a whole lot about fighting because

1-800-4-A-CHILD
www.callingallhearts.com

of getting beaten all the time. One of the things I picked up on pretty quickly was to watch the other person's eyes. Right before they hit you, their eyes would start getting bigger. Once I learned this, I became an even better fighter.

I was so good that people started avoiding me. I went everywhere to find a fight, but people would leave when they would see me. I really started enjoying fighting; I could give back without having to take it all the time. I kept feeling like my dad was surely going to kill me for all the fights I was getting into, but to be honest, I just didn't care. I thought I would probably be better off dead. I started wondering what death would be like. I asked myself, *Should I just kill somebody to see what it's like?*

My heart just wasn't set on murder unless it was mine or my father's. *I'll probably be dead by the time I'm thirty*, I thought. I figured it might as well be now. Life was getting tougher by the day. I always had to work after school and usually didn't get home until after ten o'clock at night and then had to do homework. I always fell asleep before I got my homework done. My grades began to decline. When my dad asked me about it, I told him it was because of incomplete homework. He decided to have my mother stay up with me to make sure I got it done. She had to get up an hour before he did every morning to be at work by seven o'clock in the morning. Naturally he wasn't going to stay up with me, which was fine with me.

The Mathews family lived right behind us. Melvin Matthews was the boy whose uncle broke my fishing pole as a kid and whose mother made me fight him. Melvin had a little brother, Timmie. Surprisingly, Timmie looked up to me, and we were good friends. Timmie was still in school in Hollister, and I was going to Chatty High School.

At our house, times were tough. Food was hard to come by. I stayed hungry all the time. Between hunger pains and pains from beatings, I was about to go crazy. I felt like that little steel ball in a pinball machine. I'd get knocked one way then the other. It was constantly happening, and my life seemed forever in turmoil.

I happened to think one day if I could get in Hollister School at night, I could get some food. I talked to Timmie and asked him to unlock a window in the lunchroom for me so I could get in the school at night. He said he would. He unlocked the window for me on a Friday.

That night, Timmie, Billy Cunningham, and I went to the school about nine o'clock. We all climbed in through the window. I had not eaten since that morning. The others had no supper, so we were all famished. We got inside and found the canned meat. It was government-issued, called commodities. They were designed for people who had no food. We opened the meat and got a knife and sliced it, putting it on bread. We went to the fridge and got some chocolate milk. We sat down at one of the lunch tables and pigged out. It felt so good to get rid of the hunger pains! This went on for seven weeks. Timmie was supposed to keep us informed if he heard anything about food missing from school.

1-800-4-A-CHILD
www.callingallhearts.com

A few months later, Timmie came to me one Saturday and said he wanted me to go to Wichita Falls, Texas, with him. It was only about thirty-five miles away. He had met some new friends, and they were going to get some beer and have some fun. I wanted to go so badly. I couldn't remember the last time I had some fun. I wanted to so badly, but I knew I couldn't.

I went to bed that night, jealous of the fun I knew Timmie was having. That next morning, my mother woke me up and said that Timmie had been killed in a car accident. I wept furiously. I got my clothes on and ran to his house. His dad met me at the door.

"Rodney!" he cried. "We lost him! My son! My boy!" He fell into my arms and sobbed. I wept too, holding Mr. Matthews in his doorway.

"I'm so, so sorry!" I said through sobs. Timmie was my friend, and I certainly didn't have many of them. I sat down at their kitchen table with Mr. Matthews, and he told me Timmie was in the backseat of a 1965 Ford Mustang. They were crossing the Red River Bridge, east of Burkburnett, Texas. They had slowed down, and a car rear-ended them.

Timmie was burned to death. I couldn't even imagine how he might have suffered. I was distraught; I wished I had been in his place. I wanted to die, but I surely didn't want a friend like Timmie to die. I was so devastated. I went back home and sat down at the kitchen table, head in my hands, crying.

My dad walked in and said, "What happened to Timmie?" I could hardly tell him for crying.

1-800-4-A-CHILD
www.callingallhearts.com

"Will you shut up?" he said. "Quit crying. They were probably drinking, and if so, he deserved to die."

"You asshole!" I screamed at him, rising from my seat. He hit me in the face with his fist. Again, I crawled inside of myself and went numb. He hit me again. I hardly felt it, as I was somewhat comatose. I spent the rest of the day in my room, crying. I was in shock that he didn't bother me anymore. I begged God again to please kill him.

I woke up in the middle of the night and decided it was time for him to die. I made my way to their bedroom and into the big closet. I searched for the .22 rifle and was shocked when I couldn't find it. It had always been in there! I made my way back to my bedroom and went back to bed.

The next day, I ran home from school to get there ahead of my sisters. I went straight to the closet and searched again for the rifle. It wasn't there. My chance at freedom was gone. I became even more depressed.

No Love at All

What was missing
In my life
Was daddy's love, which there
Never was enough of.

In fact there was
Never any at all.
It was like running

1-800-4-A-CHILD
www.callingallhearts.com

Head-on into a wall.

No matter how I tried,
If I said he loved me,
I knew I had lied.
I was dying inside.

People ask me,
"How did you survive?"
The love of my wife's family
Is what kept me alive.

Chapter Seventeen

My life was a deep, dark hole of depression. Every morning I woke up, I felt more and more defeated. Then, as a freshman, I got to meet a girl in the eighth grade by the name of Shauna Gale Patton. She was like a breath of fresh air. She was extremely beautiful and the kindest person I had ever met. She was my third angel. If it had not been for her, I'm sure I would have been dead or in prison.

She was such a joy to be around. I could actually laugh and have a good time with her. This was new for me; my life had been very crowded with heartache and pain. Now, life didn't seem to be nearly as bad as it was. Trust me, I still had my bad days with my dad, but finally there was something to look forward to. Whenever I would get invited to her house, I felt like I was on cloud nine. When she'd invite me over for dinner, for some reason, I would never eat. I would be starving and wouldn't eat a bite. I guess I was just so nervous. I had never been around people like her or her parents; they were such nice, good people.

At that time, my dad was working road construction in Weatherford, Oklahoma. The night before he headed out, he started loading his tools in his 1-ton truck. I, of course, was ordered to help him. Needless to say, my anxieties were high. I knew I could never do anything right for him. He was

1-800-4-A-CHILD
www.callingallhearts.com

always yelling and screaming at me for not doing things "the right way". I knew this night would be no different.

I couldn't put anything in his truck the right way. As I was putting an electric drill in the back, I felt his hand smack me across the face. It busted my lip open and blood flowed. He began screaming at me to get in the house. I made my way into the bathroom and grabbed a wash cloth. I got it wet, and started to wipe away the blood. He walked in and started screaming at me because he said I was ruining the wash cloth.

"You dumbass! Use toilet paper to wipe off blood!" he yelled. I dropped the cloth and grabbed toilet paper. My hands were still wet, so the paper stuck to them. It wasn't sopping up the blood at all. I just stuck the toilet paper in my mouth to soak up the blood in my mouth. Thankfully, he left when he saw that.

"Vida!" I heard him yell to my mother. "Get my clothes! I ain't driving sixty miles for a pair of pants."

I breathed a temporary sigh of relief. I was so glad that he would be gone. I knew I just needed to get through these last few hours with him. I hurried toward the back door where his tools were sitting, knowing he wouldn't let a bloody lip stop me from helping him.

I saw his tool box and decided to go ahead and load it. As I picked it up, I didn't think about how heavy it was going to be. I carried that box out the back door, down the steps, and to the back of his truck. I had to lift it another foot to get it into his truck. Thank God I made it. I walked back to the door to meet him.

1-800-4-A-CHILD
www.callingallhearts.com

"Where is my tool box?" he snarled.

"I loaded it myself," I replied.

"You dumbass! You could have hurt yourself!" he yelled at me.

So I can't hurt myself, but you can hurt me? I thought. I didn't say anything to him, though. I willed myself to get through the rest of this. Finally, about thirty minutes later, he was on his way to Weatherford. I felt my stomach unclench. I could finally sleep.

Our town was notorious for being riddled with stray dogs. People must've thought that since Hollister was in "the country" that the dogs they dumped wouldn't be a nuisance. How wrong they were.

On this particular day, someone had dropped two greyhounds down the street around dinnertime. I decided those stray dogs needed to be run out of town. So I proceeded to do just that. I was so upset with these dogs that I wanted to kill them. Naturally, I couldn't catch those greyhounds; they were some fast dogs. Thankfully though, I scared them enough to get them out of town.

As I walked toward the house, I saw my mother with her hands on her hips, staring at me. "What the hell do you think you're doing?" she snapped.

"Ridding the town of two more stray dogs," I said.

"You stupid son of a bitch," she said.

I was sick of it. I was tired of my father beating me and of her so I started giving it back to her, without thinking of the consequences.

1-800-4-A-CHILD
www.callingallhearts.com

"Dad talks to me like that right before he beats me, you going to do that too?" I shouted.

I saw the color rising in her cheeks. "I'm calling your father," she said through gritted teeth.

"Fine," I said. I figured he'd tell my mother to put me on the phone and I'd have to listen to his yelling for a few minutes. I had no idea what was in store for me. I followed my mother inside and listened as she told my dad what happened. When she hung up, she turned toward me and all the color had drained from her face.

"Oh my God," she said. "Rodney...he's drunk. What are we going to do?" she asked.

"What did he say?" I asked, starting to get a gnawing feeling in my stomach.

"He told me to come to Weatherford and bring you with me," she said. "What are we going to do?"

"Might as well go there," I said, knowing it was no use trying to hide or fight. "Or else he'll just come here."

She was scared; I saw the fear in her eyes. I thought if we went up there, at least there would be people around and maybe he wouldn't beat me. So my mother and two sisters loaded up in the Chevy pickup. We started our way north toward Weatherford. It was quiet in the vehicle, except for when someone would vocalize how scared they were.

"Don't worry," I told them. "He's just mad at me."

It was already dark as we started up Highway 54. Somewhere between Cooperton and Gotebo, we met my father. He was driving a service truck and spotted us. He spun around quickly and pulled in front of the pickup. My sisters started screaming and my mother was crying. We all knew his capabilities when he was drunk.

We parked on the side of Highway 54; his truck in front of us. He staggered out of the driver's side and walked toward us. He pointed his finger straight at me then curled it back, meaning he wanted me to come to him. I opened the door, climbed out and started toward him.

When I got between the two pickups, he hit me in the face with his fist as hard as he could. I hit the pavement, stunned. He yelled at me to get up. I was moving too slow for him, so he kicked me as hard as he could. I rolled away from him quickly and got to my knees. I saw his fist coming right at my face. My reaction time was slowing down; I couldn't block his punches.

He jerked me up to my feet and hit me in the face. I fell to the pavement again. As I'm lying there, too dazed to speak, I saw a barbwire fence a few feet from the road. I thought I might be able to hop that fence and runaway. I couldn't gather my thoughts fast enough before he kicked me in the stomach.

God please make him stop, I thought.

But my father didn't stop. He kept going. I later heard my sisters say he hit me, non-stop for an hour and a half. I heard my sisters and mother screaming and crying from the pickup. I knew they were scared. I was too. Finally, he told me to get my ass up and in his pickup.

I couldn't see, so I felt around on the ground, fumbling for the pickup. I opened the door and sat down in the seat. I heard my father start his truck. I tried opening my eyes but I couldn't; they were swollen shut. We started to drive back on the road. He started yelling at me, calling me a stupid son of a bitch.

"You're on drugs aren't you?" he accused. "The whole damn town of Hollister is on drugs!"

He hit me with the back of his hand on the back of my head. I started to cry; the pain was absolutely horrible. For the next thirty minutes, he hit me alternating between my face and stomach. I tried to put my arms in the way of his fist. Even though I couldn't see his hands, I could try to anticipate his moves. He beat me all the way back to his place in Weatherford. By the time we pulled in, I was almost lifeless.

"I'm not taking him in there, Vida," I heard my dad say to my mom. I knew why he didn't want me to go inside. He shared that trailer with another guy that worked in Weatherford and he didn't want any witnesses.

I felt my dad drag me out of the truck; I walked like I was drunk. I heard him open the tailgate of the truck and felt him push me against it. "Get your dumb ass up in the back of this pickup," he snarled.

I couldn't see and so I slipped. Then I felt a hard kick against my legs. I screamed out in pain. He yelled at me to shut up and I felt my way into the truck.

"Lay down!" my father yelled. I obeyed. I heard the crinkle of an old tarp and felt the heavy plastic fall over me.

"If you try to leave or if you make a sound, I swear I'll kill you," he said.

I wish you would, I thought. *Then I'd finally be free of you.*

I honestly didn't care if I died. It had to be better than what he put me through. Soon after, my mother woke me up to tell me we were going home. My face, head, and stomach all were sore and throbbing. I heard my dad walk over and say: "You'd better mind from now on, boy."

My mother and sisters helped me into the pickup and we headed back home. I could hear their sniffles as we drove. They started to talk about what to do now. My sisters kept saying: "We need to leave. We need out of here!"

"It won't work," I said, startling my sisters. "He'll track us down and kill every one of us."

"He would," I heard my mother whisper. We knew then that there was no hope. We all started to cry. I tried not to because the tears burned my swollen eyes so much. I felt the pickup start to slow and I knew we were pulling into the driveway. "Wait here," I heard my mother say. She got out of the car and returned minutes later. "Help me girls," she said to my sisters.

I felt the softness of a quilt wrap around me, covering me from head to foot. My mother and sisters led me inside. They didn't want any neighbors seeing me beaten to a pulp.

They sat me down on the couch and I felt a pillow being placed under my head. Someone turned on the TV, even though I couldn't see the program. I fell asleep, not waking until the next afternoon. My mother woke me gently, but I sat upright because I heard my father's voice from the other room.

1-800-4-A-CHILD
www.callingallhearts.com

He's here to kill me, I thought. I was okay with that, though, because to me life was no longer worth living. I didn't care anymore. I heard footsteps near me and I tensed up. Not being able to see him scared me.

"I guess now you will be a good little boy," I heard him say.

I felt the anger rage within. How dare he say that to me? I decided right then, he had to die. There was no remorse in his voice; he didn't care about me. No matter the cost, I had to kill him.

I started making plans to make this happen. I told myself that when I was able to get up and around, I was going to load the .22-riffle in the closet and leave it there until he came home again. Then, while he was asleep, I would kill him. I had had enough; I couldn't take it anymore.

The next day, my mother and sisters went to Fredrick. I was left alone. I had been unable to eat the past two days. I felt my way to the bathroom. I started to throw up. I slowly pried one of my eyes open and saw blood in the toilet. My stomach sank. I thought I might be dying. I slowly stood up and made myself look at my reflection in the mirror. I was not ready for that. Seeing my face, bloodied and beaten, I was even more resolved to kill my father.

I felt my way back to the TV room and lay down. I felt for the telephone and found it, searching for the numbers to call my girlfriend, Shauna. I told her I got jumped in Frederick; beaten by three guys. I was too ashamed to tell her the truth. I wanted her to know I was going to be down for a while.

A couple of hours later, my mother and sisters came home from Frederick. My mother was beside herself. She had heard from somebody that I said I got beat up in Frederick.

"Why would you do that?" she yelled.

"Isn't that better than telling the truth? Just in case somebody saw me, they'd know what happened," I said.

"If anybody finds out, I'll tell your daddy to have at you again," she said menacingly.

"You better not," I said, squaring my shoulders. "Or you'll regret it."

"What does that mean?" she asked.

"Figure it out yourself," I replied.

"You're full of shit," my mother said.

"Yeah? Just watch me."

During this time, I had a job of cutting and bailing hay. After the beating, my boss kept calling my house, looking for me. My mother told him I was gone helping my dad. By the third day home, I was able to eat a little and get the swelling down. Two weeks later you could hardly tell that I was almost beaten to death.

The next week I went back to my job of cutting and bailing hay. The first night I was getting in an alfalfa patch with my boss and I decided to tell him the truth about what happened to me. He just said, "Well, that's too bad."

I could not believe my ears. I just told this guy that my own father almost killed me and that's all he can say? He obviously didn't believe me. I thought he liked me and would help me...boy, was I ever wrong.

Why, Dad, Why?

If I could just ask a few questions,
I wonder to this day,
Why did you beat me
And have such cruel things to say?

~

Why did you have to start
When I was only three,
When you kicked me so hard
And brought me to my knees?

~

Why did you not care
About all my pain?
What did you think
You really had to gain?

~

Was I just the object
Of your frustrations in life,
That you had to beat me
Within an inch of my life?

~

I tried to love you,
But you never cared,

1-800-4-A-CHILD
www.callingallhearts.com

Because if you had,
The beatings would have been spared.

You created hate in me
That I never dreamed of.
It would never have been rooted
If you would have shown just a trace of any kind of love.

Why did you break my heart
And break my will?
Did it somehow make you feel good
To see my blood spill?

Did it make you feel good to fill
My life with fear,
Or just make you thirsty
For another cold beer?

I tried my best to be
Your perfect son,
But why did you beat me
When I tried to have fun?

1-800-4-A-CHILD
www.callingallhearts.com

There was a time when I just wanted
You to kill me to end the fight,
Because you had convinced me that
I could never be right.

I guess you were drunk.
I could explain it away,
But the fact was, when you were sober,
You were the same way.

Why was I beaten
Until I couldn't be recognized?
Why was I always hated
And truly despised?

Why was it important to you
To see me as a loser?
Was it because in your finest hour
You were just a boozer?

If it weren't for my three angels
I wouldn't be alive,

So why were you so anxious
To see me die?

So I must ask this question
Just one more time:
"What in the world were you thinking?"
And, "Why, Dad, Why?"

Chapter Eighteen

The road construction company my dad worked for moved their offices all the time. In the fall of that year, the company moved near Idabel. It was getting close to Christmastime, so my mother decided that we would go to Idabel to spend Christmas with Dad. I couldn't believe it. I was so distraught. I wanted to be close to Shauna, but no such luck.

We all loaded into the car and went to Idabel. It was about a seven-hour drive. We were out of school for ten days; I dreaded, with passion, having to be around my dad that long. Upon arrival at the construction plant, my mother told my dad something was wrong with the car. It was a 1965 Malibu with a standard transmission. Dad drove it and came back and said the clutch was going out. So he got on the phone and ordered parts. The next day, the parts arrived, and my mother wanted to go to Ada to her mother's for Christmas. My dad told her she could drive his pickup and take Shirley and Carolyn with her, but I had to stay to help put the clutch in the car.

My heart sank. I was hoping to get to go with my mom and sisters, to get away from my dad. Since the construction company shut down for the holidays, my dad brought the car up there and used the tools and ramps to fix it. Actually, *I* fixed it.

There was a scale house on the construction site. The small building was heated and was just outside the ramp to the scales. Dad had me pull the car onto the ramp and then jump down in the hollow area of the ramp, underneath the car. Then, Dad sat in the building where it was warm. I was under the car, freezing my butt off. He talked through a small window and told me everything to do. I kept motivating myself: *Get it fixed so you can get home and see Shauna.*

Three hours later, I was done. Dad drove it and said it was working well. He hit me in the chest with his fist.

"What was that for?" I asked.

"For taking too long," he said.

"That was my first clutch!" I said.

He backhanded me and knocked me to the floor. I got up and walked out of the building and went to the trailer house he lived in. I feel asleep on the couch. My mother and sisters were home by noon. We were all setting at the kitchen table, and my mother started talking about all my cousins that were in college, telling my dad what they were majoring in.

"Did you tell them what your son was majoring in?" he asked.

"What?" my mother asked, confused.

"He's majoring in 'do you want to step outside,'" said my dad, chuckling to himself.

Does he not know he created a monster? I thought.

Honestly, I don't think he ever figured it out. He was always degrading me for something. After dinner, he got up and went to his closet. He pulled the .22 rifle out and said,

"I'm going hunting." That was the gun I had been looking for! We left for the house the next day. I was so relieved! I was finally getting back to my girl, Shauna.

The next weekend, Dad was back at home. He had me up by seven o'clock in the morning, working outside. He made me use a high-lift jack to pick up the front of a wrecked truck. They were not stable at all, but I was strong and could get enough leverage on it to keep it from falling.

All of a sudden I heard my dad yelling. "Let that jack down, or you're going to lose your damn hand!"

"I got this," I reassured him. I knew what I was doing.

I soon felt his hands shove against my back, and I fell to the ground. The jack fell also. I was done. I got up and went inside. I passed my mother, who had been standing inside watching us.

"He was just trying to keep you from losing your hand," she said.

"I'd rather lose a hand than listen to that crap," I said.

I decided I didn't want to go inside. He'd just come in and get me. I walked down the driveway and down the highway. I heard the rumble of his truck behind, but I didn't look up.

"Get in," he hollered to me.

"I want to be left alone," I hollered back, not looking at him. I knew I didn't have any place to go, but I didn't care.

He followed me for a while longer, telling me to get in the car. I started shivering from the cold and finally relented. Of course, the whole ride home, he lectured me about the jack.

1-800-4-A-CHILD
www.callingallhearts.com

All I could think was, *I would much rather only have* one *hand than have to deal with this.*

When it got a little warmer outside, the family started going to the stock car races at Lawton Motor Speedway. I got hooked quickly. I loved watching the cars race, the smell of the exhaust, and the loud roar of the engines. It was nice to be able to zone out and do something fun for once.

One day I talked to a friend of mine, Dennis Wilson. He was actually my sister Carolyn's boyfriend. We pooled our money together and bought a '49 Chevy from "Old Man Miller" on the south side of town. They had started a new hobby-stock class in Lawton, and we were going to race in the new class.

Dennis and I spent six weeks getting our car ready. Finally, we were ready to race. We spent every dime we had and sold everything we could to get this car ready to race. We needed twenty dollars to buy gas to get there and for our pit passes. We exhausted every effort to raise the money; we were flat broke.

I got up the nerve to ask my dad, who had actually showed an interest in the car while we were building it. The first words out of his mouth were, "Not *no*. But, *hell no*."

I left brokenhearted and dejected. I wanted to race so badly, but as usual, there was no support from him. I remember thinking, *It must be the drinking that is causing all this.* It was worse when he was drinking, but, truly, it happened more when he was sober.

I started spending as much time with Shauna as I could. She was my solace. She made me feel protected, whole, and warm. We started dating regularly: to the movies, football games in Frederick, food in Lawton—just wherever we could get away from everyone. We became very close, and within a short period of time we started having sex. Not too long after that, she found out she was pregnant, even though we were using protection.

We knew we were going to have to face our parents; I think that terrified us more than thinking about raising a child. As bad as it was, Shauna's parents, Leston and Janella, were mature and full of love. We discussed options with them. We decided we would get married, which meant *both* sets of parents would have to sign for us to do that.

I left a note one day for my parents, not wanting to die. My dad acknowledged the letter, and my mother started screaming and yelling at me. My mother went with me, Shauna, and her mom to Lawton to sign the paperwork. I know it hurt Shauna's parents, but they were so kind and understanding.

The wedding was set for January 31, 1970. I was the ripe old age of sixteen, and she was fifteen. That little baby that Shauna had growing in her belly saved my life. I was so close to murdering my father, even I couldn't believe it. We moved into a small two-room house, behind Shauna's parents. After our honeymoon, we went to my house to get my clothes. My mother threw them all out on the front porch. I apologized to Shauna as we picked them up and went back to her parents' house.

I was depressed. I tried to figure out why my parents hated me. Finally, my mother came clean and said she was embarrassed that I got Shauna pregnant and married her. If *anybody* should have been embarrassed, it should have been Shauna's parents. They were very well-respected people. But they were the ones who were very understanding.

Later that year, on June 13, 1970, our son Randy was born. It was an amazing experience. When I saw that little boy for the first time, I swore I'd never treat him like my dad did me. I wanted to be a good dad, not a fear-inducing one. Randy was very precious to everyone—more so to Shauna's family than to mine.

About a year and a half later, Shauna and I were over at my mom and dad's house. Shirley, Carolyn, Shauna, and I worked at a plant in Frederick known as Kellwood's. Nobody could get to work because it was solid ice. My mom and dad had gone to the local café.

Shirley had married a guy named Glen Wilson. Glen was a big ole boy; he played football at Frederick High School and was extremely strong. I had tried him a couple of times and could not beat him. He was about six feet tall and weighed three hundred pounds. I was six two and weighed 185. During that fight, I had marked his face up pretty good but could not get the better of him.

While we were at my parents' house, Glen told Shirley to go make him some macaroni and cheese. She told him if he wanted some to fix it himself. He got up from the table and walked to where she was and hit her in the face.

I jumped up and told Shauna to go to the other end of the house where our son was sleeping. I ran outside and hopped in my vehicle, speeding on the ice to the café. I burst in and found my dad.

"You need to get home," I told him. "Glen just hit Shirley in the face."

My parents got up and ran to my dad's truck. When we got there, Glen and Shirley were in my old bedroom, yelling at each other. My dad went in there and told Glen to go in the other room and cool off. Glen was about to go overseas for the air force and had bought Shirley a .22 pistol. It was laying on a bookshelf in a box in the room where they were fighting.

I could hear Glen and my dad yelling at each other. Then I heard Shirley scream out, "Daddy! That gun is *loaded*!" That got my attention. They came out of that room with the gun stuck in my dad's face. I didn't think; I just reacted.

I went up over Glen's back and wrapped my right hand around the barrel. I pulled that pistol straight up, and with my hand around the barrel, he fired it twice. The bullets went straight through the ceiling. I jerked the gun away from him. It felt like my hand was on fire.

When I got the gun, Glen stopped fighting. As he started toward the door, I pulled on the trigger. It wouldn't budge. I looked, and the safety was off. I stuck it to the back of his head, and the trigger would not pull. At the same time, my dad and I kicked him square in the butt. He went flying off the front porch on his face. He went to his parents' house, and my dad went to Frederick to the sheriff's department and filled out a report.

Three weeks later, he was fined twenty-five dollars for disturbing the peace. I thought to myself, *This is no place to raise a family*. Shauna's parents had moved to Oklahoma City a few years before; they decided they were done with farming. She and I took Randy and went to visit her parents. I needed out of that place. I was sick of my parents and all their drama and violence.

A Mother's Love

Does anyone really
Know me at all?
Have I failed
To answer the call?

What would I have
Been in this life
If I hadn't been abused?
Did it make me quit? I refused.

Did I ever wanna quit?
It felt like I was run over and hit!
A young man with so much pain
It was driving me insane!

1-800-4-A-CHILD
www.callingallhearts.com

Burning inside, to help
All people all of the time.
Confused, because truly
I didn't have a dime.

I begged, borrowed, and stole
To give other people a chance.
I couldn't rid myself of that
Effort to make that stance.

I've always known
I have to follow my heart
Or I would personally
Dwindle and fall apart.

It kept driving me
To do things I shouldn't.
Trying to stop it,
Sorry I couldn't.

I was an angry young man
Because of the abuse that I had.

1-800-4-A-CHILD
www.callingallhearts.com

To see people in need
Made me extremely sad.

Mixed emotions, so confused
I tried but still wound up bruised,
Pushed inside to help someone.
No money, I felt I should run!

I made so many mistakes,
People still don't forgive.
Wonder if they could have made it.
If they had to live like I had to live?

That burning desire to help
Would not ever go away,
Broke and overwhelmed
Wasn't sure I could stay.

Fought this battle
Over and over, day after day,
Unable to help people in need
When all around me was pure greed.

1-800-4-A-CHILD
www.callingallhearts.com

I, myself, struggled dramatically
With my past,
Asking God every day,
Will I make it? Will I last?

Why was I thrown
In the middle of this fight?
Was it because
My heart wasn't right?

You should know I always gave,
Even when I didn't have it to give.
I couldn't watch people suffer.
Was I wrong?
Aren't we supposed to help one another?

People ask me, "What would have made your life easier? It
was obvious your dad hated you." The one thing people don't
think of was that it would have made my life easier if my
mother would have really been there for me. Never under-
estimate the need for a mother's true love. It has the power
of changing and molding their children's hearts and lives! It
creates inner confidence that makes their lives always thrive!

1-800-4-A-CHILD
www.callingallhearts.com

Make no mistake; a mother's love has the power to get you through practically anything in your life. You might ask why the mother? Because they are the closest example we have to God's love here on earth. True fact, I know as I never got it myself and I realized the value. No, I don't want your sympathy! If you are a parent, love your children with all your heart! We can change this country overnight if you would just do your part.

1-800-4-A-CHILD
www.callingallhearts.com

About the Author

Rodney Timms works with organizations such as the Oklahoma Institute for Child Advocacy (OICA) and Childhelp® to raise awareness about child abuse and to support prevention efforts. He has written a book, *Calling All Hearts*, full of descriptive poems reliving his personal childhood abuse from ages four to fifteen when his father almost beat him to death. Timms is president of Western Flyer Express, an Oklahoma City based national trucking company with 250 trucks and 500 trailers that have Childhelp® National Child Abuse Hotline on the back of each of them calling for action to help children. In 2011, he wrapped one of his tractor trailers in the OICA "Protect Kids" campaign logo and displays it at CAP Day at the State Capitol and at other events. He recently presented Gov. Fallin with a replica of the truck, and he donates T-shirts with the replica's image and OICA campaign slogan to sell with all proceeds going to OICA. This year he donated diapers for the CAP Day Diaper drive to benefit the Infant Crisis Services in Oklahoma City, lifesavers and cards for child advocates to give to legislators, and supplies for various child abuse prevention programs. Timms challenges all Oklahomans to get involved and make a difference in the life of a child.

If I made it, you can too. You've got to stay positive! It *is* possible to make it through any type of abuse with sheer

1-800-4-A-CHILD
www.callingallhearts.com

determination and God's love. Remember: never ever give up!
My story will be continued in my next book, *Contract Killer*.

1-800-4-A-CHILD
www.callingallhearts.com

Achievments

2012 Marion Jacewitz Award Winner

The Marion Jacewitz Award is presented to an individual Oklahoman who made significant contributions to the prevention of child abuse on a staewide level. To be considered for this award an individual must participate in at least one creative and innovative chld abuse prevention program, have demonstrated leadership in promoting the prevention of child abuse statewide, have demonstrated commitment to improving the quality of life for children and their families, and have also been invloved in the field of child abuse prevention for at least two years.

2009 Childhelp Founders' Award

The beautiful and compassionate heart of our beloved friend Rodney Timms has comforted countless children in our care. He continues to be a knight in shinning armor to these hurting little ones with his unwavering loyalty, gallant generosity, and noble spirit.

Rodney is himself a survivor of child abuse and an inspiration to everyone associated with Childhelp. He is a hero of epic proportions who has triumphed over unimaginable darkness and adversity. Against tremendous odds he rose above his painful childhood and became a God-send to us and to all of the little lives he has touched.

Thank you Rodney for sharing your story - your courage inspires every one of us to reach higher, work harder, and nerver lct go of our shared vision to see child abuse and neglet eradicated. God bless you, friend!

—Sara O'Meara & Yvonne Fredderson

Photos

The Church where we were married. Jan. 31, 1970.

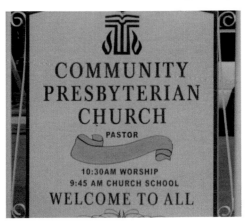

1-800-4-A-CHILD
www.callingallhearts.com

Chattanooga Public Schools.

Chattanooga Public School

The Brick in the sidewalk at Chattanooga Public School.

1-800-4-A-CHILD
www.callingallhearts.com

The Activity Center & Gym at Chattanooga Public School.

The small house we lived in from 1971–1972.

The Bar in Chattanooga where my Dad hungout.

Shauna's Parents House.

The small 2 room house we lived in from January 1970–1971.

*The house where my friends Jerry & Ronnie
Kimbell lived in Frederick, OK.*

*The grain elevator in Hollister, OK where
I worked while in high school.*

*This is what's left of the old gin tank, where
my first angel saved me from drowning.*

1·800-4-A-CHILD
www.callingallhearts.com

One of three grain elevators in Hollister, OK.

The Cunningham house – Hollister, OK.

Melvin & Timmie Matthews home in Hollister, OK.

The house I lived in, from 6–16, in Hollister, OK.

The shop building my dad would beat me in.

My dad's truck shop.

The house where Hunk Rich lived when he was killed. Later became my dad's truck shop.

My sister Carolyn's house. This is the site where the Blair house sat when Hunk Rich was stabbed to death.

1-800-4-A-CHILD
www.callingallhearts.com

The First Baptist Church in Hollister, OK.

This is what is left of Hollisters Public School. I attended school here from 1st through 8th grade.

The gas station building in Hollister, OK. I remember gas was 15 cents per gallon.

Our house in Frederick, OK. We lived here until I was 5.

Frederick Clinic where I was born Sept. 17, 1953.

*This is where Jerry & Jimmy Hendricks
Lived in Frederick, OK.*

The road sign going into Chattanooga, OK.